WHY DO
DOGS
LIKE BALLS?

WHY DO
DOGS
LIKE BALLS?

More Than 200 Canine Quirks,
Curiosities, and Conundrums Revealed

D. CAROLINE COILE, PhD
AND
MARGARET H. BONHAM

STERLING

New York / London
www.sterlingpublishing.com

STERLING and the distinctive Sterling logo are
registered trademarks of Sterling Publishing Co., Inc.

Library of Congress Cataloging-in-Publication Data

Coile, D. Caroline.
  Why do dogs like balls? ; more than 200 canine quirks, curiosities, and conundrums
revealed / D. Caroline Coile and Margaret H. Bonham.
      p. cm.
  Includes index.
  ISBN 978-1-4027-5039-7
  1. Dogs--Behavior--Miscellanea. 2. Dogs--Miscellanea. I. Bonham, Margaret H. II.
Title.
  SF433.C643 2008
  636.7--dc22
                                                                    2008018840

10 9 8 7 6 5 4 3 2 1

Published by Sterling Publishing Co., Inc.
387 Park Avenue South, New York, NY 10016
© 2008 by Margaret H. Bonham and D. Caroline Coile, Ph.D.
Distributed in Canada by Sterling Publishing
c/o Canadian Manda Group, 165 Dufferin Street
Toronto, Ontario, Canada M6K 3H6
Distributed in the United Kingdom by GMC Distribution Services
Castle Place, 166 High Street, Lewes, East Sussex, England BN7 1XU
Distributed in Australia by Capricorn Link (Australia) Pty. Ltd.
P.O. Box 704, Windsor, NSW 2756, Australia

Sterling ISBN 978-1-4027-5039-7

For information about custom editions, special sales, premium and
corporate purchases, please contact Sterling Special Sales
Department at 800-805-5489 or specialsales@sterlingpublishing.com.

CONTENTS

1. DOG BEHAVIOR   1

Do other dogs think Poodles are aliens?   2
Do dogs believe pictures of dogs are real?   2
Do dogs recognize themselves in the mirror?   3
Why do dogs chase cats?   4
Why do some dogs chase cars?   4
Are dogs that kill animals likely to turn on people?   5
If a puppy sucks its food instead of lapping it,
    does it mean it's aggressive?   6
Why do dogs bark?   6
Are debarked dogs frustrated?   8
Why do male dogs cock their leg?   9
Can female dogs cock their legs?   10
Why do dogs lick people?   10
Why do dogs jump up on people?   11
Is rolling a dog over on its back a good way
    to show him who's alpha?   12
Are yawns contagious to dogs?   13
Why do dogs smell other dogs' butts?   13
Why do dogs sniff poop or pee?   13
Why do some dogs eat doo-doo?   14
Why do dogs eat plants, dirt, wool, and other weird stuff?   15
Why do dogs bury bones?   16
Why do dogs rub on disgusting stuff?   17
Why do dogs scoot on their butts?   18
Why do dogs cock their head?   18
Why do dogs wag their tail?   19
Do dogs with docked tails miss them?   20

Why do dogs turn in a circle before they lie down?   20

Why do dogs howl with sirens?   21

Why are some dogs afraid of thunder?   21

Can dogs have mental illness?   22

Can dogs be born bad?   23

Can dogs be obsessive compulsive?   23

Why do dogs chase their tails?   24

Why do dogs like to hang their head out of car windows?   25

Can dogs get amnesia?   26

Can dogs have narcolepsy?   26

Can dogs be hypnotized?   27

Why do some dogs go into a trance when they walk under leaves?   28

Can dogs become comatose?   28

Do dogs like to be hugged?   29

Why do dogs go crazy after a bath?   29

How do dogs know it's time for dinner?   30

How do dogs know it's time for a walk?   30

Why do dogs like balls?   31

2. CANINE INTELLIGENCE   33

Do dogs think?   34

Do dogs with little heads have little brains and little minds?   35

Is there such a thing as phrenology for dogs?   36

Do dogs remember incidents?   37

Are some breeds really that dumb?   37

Can dogs be mentally deficient?   40

Can dogs count?   41

Do dogs know calculus?   42

Do dogs understand it when you point?   42

Can dogs learn to read?   43

Can some foods make dogs smarter?   44

Do dogs understand the concept of time?   45

Do dogs get Alzheimer's?   45

3. THE DOG'S EMOTIONS   47

Do dogs mourn?   48

Can you trust someone your dog hates?   49

Do dogs have friends and enemies?   50

Do dogs feel jealousy and spite?   50

Do dogs fall in love?   51

Do dogs cry?   52

Do dogs have a sense of humor
    (and can they play practical jokes)?   53

Do dogs get embarrassed?   53

4. THE CANINE BODY   55

Do rabid dogs really foam at the mouth?   56

Do dogs blush?   57

Do old dogs get gray hair?   58

Can dogs be albinos?   58

Do dogs get sunburned?   59

Do some dogs have higher body temperatures than others?   60

Does shaving a dog's fur make him cooler?   60

Do dogs sweat?   61

Do dogs get pimples?   63

Do dogs get goose bumps?   63

Do dogs get warts?   64

Do dogs have belly buttons?   65

Can a dog's eye really pop out of his head?   65

Can dogs suck out of a straw?   66

Why don't dogs get hairballs?   66

Do dogs get tonsillitis?   66

Do dogs get appendicitis?   67

Do dogs catch colds?   67

Do dogs get the flu?   67

Why do dogs get gas so often?   68

Does a dog's stomach rumble when he's hungry?   69

Can dogs be right pawed or left-pawed?   69

Can dogs break their collarbone?   70

Why do dogs have wet noses?   70

Do dogs get boogers?   70

Can you tickle a dog?7   71

Do dogs get hiccups?   71

Do dogs' legs ever fall asleep?   72

Do dogs snore?   72

Does sugar make dogs hyperactive?   72

Can dogs have low blood sugar?   73

Will a convulsing dog swallow his tongue?   74

Do dogs ever bite their own tongue?   75

Can a dog live without a tongue?   75

Are some dogs' bites more dangerous than others'?   76

Are dogs with blue eyes blind, deaf, or crazy?   76

Why are dogs' eyes reflective, and do the
    colors mean anything?   77

Can all dogs swim?   78

Can dogs swim underwater?   78

Is the fastest dog faster than the fastest horse?   79

What's the purpose of that footpad way up at the top of
    the dog's wrist?   79

Can dogs have extra toes, like some cats do?   80

Do some dogs have webbed feet?   *80*

How do three-legged dogs get around?   *81*

Can a dog with only two legs get around?   *81*

Do all big dogs have bad hips?   *81*

Why are some breeds' tails docked?   *82*

Does docking a dog's tail throw off his balance?   *83*

Does it hurt puppies when their tails are docked?   *83*

Why don't breeders just breed tailless dogs
    if that's what they want?   *85*

Is one dog year equal to seven people years?   *86*

Will dog spit kill you faster than human spit?   *87*

Are some dogs sneeze-free—for allergic people?   *88*

Are some breeds really single-coated?   *89*

Why do some dogs shed and others don't?   *90*

How do sled dogs sleep in the snow without freezing?   *91*

How do dogs run on snow without their feet freezing?   *92*

How can dogs run a thousand miles or more in sledding
    competitions?   *93*

Can dogs be blood donors?   *94*

Do dogs have different blood types?   *95*

5. A DOG'S SENSES   97

Can dogs smell fear?   *98*

Can dogs smell the difference between identical twins?   *98*

When a dog tracks somebody and starts in the middle,
    how does he know which way to go?   *99*

Can dogs sniff out cancer?   *101*

Can a dog be scent-blind?   *102*

Can dogs recognize seizures before they happen?   *103*

How good is a dog's sense of smell?   *104*

Do "dog-appeasing pheromones" work?   105

Why do some dogs chomp and foam at the mouth when
    they smell the urine of other dogs?   106

Does pepper spray work on dogs?   106

How good is a dog's eyesight?   107

Can dogs see color, or do they just see in black and white?   107

Do dogs' eyes glow when they get angry?   108

Can dogs with hair over their eyes see?   109

Do dogs need glasses?   109

Do old dogs need bifocals?   110

Do some breeds have better eyesight than others?   111

Can dogs watch TV?   111

If a dog has his lens removed because of cataracts,
    should he have a fake one put back in?   112

What's a third eyelid?   113

Are blind dogs sad?   113

Do dogs need hearing aids?   114

Is it dangerous to live with a deaf dog?   115

Do deaf Dalmatians make better fire dogs because
    the sirens don't bother them?   115

Do silent dog whistles work?   116

Can dogs hear those ultrasonic pest deterrents?   116

Does cropping a dog's ears make him hear better?   117

How do dogs taste their food when they gulp it down so fast?   117

Do dogs like artificial sweeteners?   118

Does a dog really need his whiskers?   118

Why are puppies born with their eyes closed?   119

Can newborn puppies see, hear, smell, or taste?   120

Can puppies smell in the womb?   121

6. THE SEXUAL DOG   123

Can dogs be homosexual?   124

Do dogs get stuck when having intercourse?   124

Can a litter have more than one father?   125

Is there such a thing as a doggy paternity test?   126

Can DNA tests tell one breed from another?   128

Can dogs be identical twins?   128

Can dogs be conjoined, like Siamese twins?   129

If a female is bred near the start of her receptive time and again
    near the end, a week later, will some puppies be born a week
    premature?   129

Can big dogs have sex with little dogs?   130

Is it dangerous to breed a little female to a much bigger male,
    because the fetus will get too big?   131

Can dogs mate with wolves, coyotes, or foxes?   131

Do dogs get sexually transmitted diseases?   132

Can a woman get pregnant from a dog?   133

Can a dog get pregnant from a man?   134

Can giving a pregnant dog calcium end up killing her?   134

Do some breeds need Caesarean sections?   135

Why do some dogs think they're pregnant when they're not?   135

Can dogs be cloned?   137

Would a cloned dog be just like the original dog?   138

7. DOG CARE   141

Why do dogs drink from toilets?   142

Why do dogs have doggy breath?   142

Why can dogs eat garbage and not get sick?   143

Can you change a dog's name?   143

Can an older dog bond with someone?   143

Are eggs good for a dog's coat?   *144*

Are table scraps OK?   *144*

Is alcohol OK for a dog?   *145*

Why do some dogs hate car rides and others love them?   *145*

If a dog kills another animal, is that dog too dangerous
    to own?   *146*

Does tomato juice work on skunk odor with dogs?   *147*

Why do dogs prefer cat food?   *148*

Can dogs die from eating onions?   *148*

Is pork bad for dogs?   *149*

Should you let your dog roam?   *150*

Can you use people shampoo on a dog?   *150*

Is homemade food good for my dog?   *151*

Can steak bones kill my dog?   *151*

Can dogs and cats really get along?   *152*

Can people get worms from dogs?   *152*

Can you get a disease from your dog?   *153*

Is chocolate really bad for dogs?   *153*

8. MORE CANINE QUESTIONS   155

Do dogs have souls and do they go to heaven?   *156*

Do all dogs come from wolves?   *156*

Can human infants be raised by wolves?   *157*

Do dogs see ghosts?   *157*

Are dogs psychic?   *158*

Do people whip sled dogs to make them run?   *158*

Do dogs really resemble their owners?   *159*

How many people are bitten by dogs every year?   *160*

Why do dogs bite people?   *160*

What's the ugliest dog?   *161*

What's the prettiest dog?   *161*

Who was the oldest dog?   *161*

How hard is the average dog bite?   *162*

How many people are killed by dogs every year?   *162*

Will plastic jugs filled with water keep dogs from pooping
  on your lawn?   *162*

Is cocoa mulch harmful to pets?   *162*

Can dogs get the plague?   *162*

Does the black pigment on the roof of a dog's mouth
  indicate anything?   *163*

9. DOG BREEDS 165

Are Malamutes or Huskies "wild" dogs?   *166*

Do some dog breeds have wolf in them?   *166*

What's the oldest breed of dog?   *167*

Can Poodles run the Iditarod?   *168*

What breeds of dog make up sled dogs?   *168*

What's the most popular dog breed?   *169*

Are Cockapoos, Peekapoos, and other designer dogs breeds?   *169*

Why are Dalmatians associated with fire departments?   *170*

Index   *171*

1

DOG BEHAVIOR

Do other dogs think Poodles are aliens?

YOU'VE SEEN THEM—dogs with the big hair and bouffant hairdos. You'd swear they came right out of the 1980s with their mullets. If there was ever a dog that didn't quite look like a dog, it'd probably have to be a Poodle. But what do other dogs think of these unusual-looking dogs? Or any unusual-looking dog, for that matter? Do they really think Poodles are aliens?

Unlike people, dogs don't rely mainly on vision to tell them what's what, but rather on a combination of how things look, sound, and especially, smell. So, while the poodle might indeed cut a very alien line, and your dog may be suitably suspicious the first time he sees one at a distance, the nose knows, and he'll figure out pretty quickly that there's a dog under that disguise.

Case in point: Maggie's Alaskan Malamute, Kiana, once saw a Yorkshire terrier running about, and instantly lunged forward to chase it as she would a rabbit. But then Kiana caught a whiff of the Yorkie, stopped dead in her tracks, and gave Maggie such an incredulous look that it could only mean: "Would you look at that? That's a dog! I didn't know they got so small!" 🐾

Do dogs believe pictures of dogs are real?

MOST DOGS DON'T APPRECIATE ART. They won't give a second glance at a Picasso, Rembrandt, or Monet, and even turn up their noses at true masterpieces that depict dogs playing poker. So when your dog seems to be staring in admiration at your drawing of a dog, does that mean he's discovered a true artist?

Dogs seem to be able to recognize certain drawings and photographs of dogs as dogs, even sometimes reacting to them as though they were real. For example, when Michael Fox (the researcher, not the actor) showed dogs a life-size painting of one of their kind, the dogs approached it cautiously, stretching forward to sniff its mouth, ears, genitals, and butt, just as they would a real dog.

Caroline had a dog that was terrified of the dog on a box of biscuits, as well as of a picture of a raccoon's face; for him, eyes were the salient feature that seemed to set him off. Maggie has had dogs react to photographs of certain dogs and not to others. And we've both seen dogs react to cutouts of dogs and even paintings of dogs on agility obstacles. But show them a photo of a landscape or even a movie star (unless it's Lassie), and all you get are yawns. 🐾

Do dogs recognize themselves in the mirror?

WHEN PUPPIES FIRST SEE THEMSELVES IN A MIRROR, they typically react as though they're meeting another puppy. They may sniff, play, bow, bark, and try to walk around and investigate the back of the mirror. With time, however, they seem to grow tired of this scentless new puppy that silently mocks them. Is it that they realize it's some sort of trick, or do they understand it's a reflection of themselves? That would be important news for scientists interested in animal thought, since the ability to recognize oneself in a mirror is frequently cited as evidence of higher-order consciousness.

Behavioral scientists study this question in human babies and animals by placing a mark on the subject's head, one he can't feel, and then watch for his reaction when he spots it in a mirror. By two years of age, human children will act surprised, then reach for the mark. Dolphins, killer whales, great apes, and elephants also investigate the mark, by turning to view it at different angles or by touching it. Dogs, alas, do not. Then again, maybe that's for the best. Think of what it could do to a Poodle's self-esteem if he realized the that dog with the goofy do was him! 🐾

Why do dogs chase cats?

THE SUN RISES, water flows downhill, and dogs chase cats: It's a force of nature. But why? Because the earth revolves around the sun, gravity makes things fall, and, um, well—why *do* dogs chase cats?

Most dogs chase cats merely for the thrill of the chase. Wild canids hunt in part by running down game, and when they see something little and furry scampering away, it excites their natural prey drive and the chase is on! Because it's the cat's natural instinct to run away from a larger predator, her instinct is to run when she sees a dog—the perfect formula for a Keystone Cops chase through your neighborhood.

Dogs that don't chase cats usually have grown up with cats or have been smacked around a couple of times by a cat that wasn't afraid of dogs. And cats that don't run usually have been raised with a dog, or at least have had experience smacking a dog around a few times.

Some breeds have a more developed prey drive than others, but don't think this means all dogs are bloodthirsty killers. Prey drive is at the core of playing, fetching, racing, herding, pointing, tracking, and even drug-sniffing. It's part of what makes a dog a dog, rather than a child in a fur suit, who would probably also chase your cat....

Why do some dogs chase cars?

SOME DOGS HAVE BIG IDEAS. You may have seen them lying in wait by the roadside until you happen along in your car, then flying out after you, barking at the wheels. It's a dangerous sport, but some dogs are risk-takers. But why do so many dogs seem enamored with such an unhealthy pastime?

Dogs that chase cars are excited by the movement of the cars—and the fact that the car is "running away" from them. The dog has tapped into his primal nature when he sees that car. You see the car;

he sees a moose or intruder running away. And the fact that it keeps on running only rewards his behavior more, as he's obviously scared it right out of his territory. So even if he doesn't return with a fender to feast on, he can still strut back home thinking he's driven off the armored intruder—pretty heady stuff for a dog. 🐾

Are dogs that kill animals likely to turn on people?

YOU'RE WALKING ALONG IN THE PARK and suddenly Fluffy lunges, pulling the leash from your grip, and trots back a few seconds later with a dead squirrel in her teeth. Your mouth goes dry; now that she's tasted blood, could she be eyeing you next?

Don't lose any sleep over it. Most dogs that kill other animals do so because of the age-old predator-prey relationship. They saw dinner hopping around, so they went shopping with their teeth. Any animal, but especially a small one, that runs away from a dog with a strong prey drive is likely to attract that instinct to chase and label itself as potential dinner.

Most dogs would rather have people serve their dinner than be served as their dinner, and they can readily tell the difference between humans and prey animals. They may chase a running person, even nip at him, but a prey-driven attack is rare. (By the way, when a dog attacks out of prey drive, he won't growl while he's doing so.) Unfortunately, dogs that are not exposed to children may have a hard time differentiating between a small fleeing child and a prey animal. Likewise, dogs that have no control once they start chasing could run down and kill a person, if the person acts enough like prey or if the dog has no inhibition about attacking people. How does one act like prey? Run away and scream—two things frightened children are apt to do.

Does that mean Fluffy has to go? No, but it does mean you need to take precautions when she's around small animals, and you also need to socialize her around calm children. And with any dog, all children should be supervised and taught never to run or scream around dogs. 🐾

If a puppy sucks its food instead of lapping it, does it mean it's aggressive?

A LONG TIME AGO, Maggie heard about a person who would euthanize puppies that came from a primitive breed that sucked their food instead of lapping at it because he thought they would be too aggressive and wolflike. Is this really the case?

The answer is complex, but basically this one behavior isn't indicative of aggression. The reality is that puppies that suck at their food are probably very young, are still sucking on mom and are a little too young for weaning. They have the concept of food coming from the pan, but haven't made the transition from sucking on mom to lapping.

This is a breeder's old wives' tale. Putting down puppies because they suck their food instead of lapping it is needless and cruel. Such a puppy is no more likely to be aggressive than any other dog. 🐾

Why do dogs bark?

WOOF, WOOF, WOOF. If you live in a neighborhood with dogs, that sound is probably not music to your ears. The dog that cries woof can be a downright nuisance, so much so that ordinances for barking dogs are commonplace in most communities.

But while barking is just part of being a dog, it isn't something you see in the dog's wild relatives. Wolves, coyotes, and foxes don't seem to bark much, if at all. So why are we so lucky?

One theory is that barking is simply an evolutionary holdover that dogs acquired quite accidentally, sort of a case of arrested development. You see, adult wild canids usually don't bark, but as adolescents they do. Over the thousands of years of domestication, dogs that hung around humans had traits that lent themselves to doing just that: hanging around with humans. Adult wolves won't do this, but adolescent wolves are more likely to. Young wolves tend to bark when they're fearful of something, perhaps to call in reinforcements. As humans started selecting dogs for tameness, we inadvertently selected dogs with more juvenile characteristics so that they would be less independent and more trainable. The result? A dog that retains juvenile characteristics throughout its adult life—a phenomenon known as *neoteny*.

Barking can be handy to humans, so people often have selected for dogs that bark to warn them of intruders. Of course, now we have dogs that bark to warn us of the presence of oxygen in the air, or other such vital information, but just wait until a burglar shows up! Some research suggests that dogs bark for all kinds of reasons—or no reason at all. This is why some researchers consider barking to be more or less without a real purpose.

Of course, you wouldn't say that if your dog alerted you to something dangerous by barking about it, or barked when he wanted to come inside or go outside. What's more, it's been Maggie's experience that some wild canines do indeed bark when in the wild. She was hiking with her husband and two Alaskan Malamutes when they chanced upon an adult coyote, which was most perturbed that they had entered his territory. He barked and charged them, exhibiting all the behavior that a dog guarding a territory would, but did not attack, having figured out that two humans and two wolfy-looking dogs were far more than he could handle by himself. Maggie suspects that if her dogs hadn't looked so much like the enemy of the coyote (the wolf), she would not have seen that reaction. So wild canines do bark, and obviously do so when threatened, suggesting that barking does have a place in their behavioral repertoire. 🐾

Are debarked dogs frustrated?

DEBARKING, THAT IS, the removal of the skin flaps on either side of a dog's larynx that causes the barking noise, is a surgical procedure called either a ventriculocordectomy or laryngotomy. Many people denounce this surgery as being cruel; after all, who can help but think of how it would feel to have our vocal chords cut? But are debarked dogs really frustrated?

Maggie has owned several dogs that had been debarked before she received them. These dogs' voices weren't silent, but sounded a bit like a raspy cough or even a softened bark. These dogs continued to bark just as much as her dogs that had normal voices. What's more, over time, their voices "grew back" as some scar tissue formed where their vocal flaps were.

While we can't psychoanalyze Maggie's dogs, it appears that the debarked dogs behaved as normally as any other dog, with no apparent behavior problems. We suspect this is largely owing to the fact that debarking doesn't make a dog silent—the dog can and does still vocalize.

Should you get your dog debarked then? The answer is definitely no, unless you are faced with putting down the dog or getting rid of him. First, you should always work at training the dog and seek a behaviorist if your dog has barking problems. Putting a dog through elective surgery such as debarking should never be done unless there is truly no other choice. But if you were a dog, would you rather be yelled at all day for barking, even possibly taken to the shelter—or have an operation to soften your voice? 🐾

Why do male dogs cock their leg?

IF YOU'VE EVER SEEN TWO INTACT, mature males meet on the street, you've seen the origin of the expression "pissing contest." One dog cocks its leg and squirts a small bit of urine on some spot, and the other does the same thing in exactly the same spot. And then they may do it again. Leg cocking to urinate is natural for most adult males in the canid family, although in some, only the dominant members of a pack may lift their leg. Leg cocking in wild canids is probably a way to deposit urine around the territory at near nose level for others of the same species. That way, no intruder can use the excuse that he never smelled it. Be thankful; many wild canids also smear their feces on posts and stumps around their territory, probably for the same reason.

Young males don't tend to start leg hiking until after they've reached sexual maturity, and even then may be well over a year of age. Before that, they just stretch forward to urinate. Even mature males will sometimes not bother to cock a leg, especially if they're urinating just to pee, rather than to mark.

It's easy to suppose that the height at which the urine is deposited sends a subtle message to the dog that has to tiptoe around to sniff it, but so far nobody has done any studies to see if the higher the mark, the more likely the smeller of it is to make a run for it. Still, it does seem that part of the pissing contest involves lifting that leg so high that the lifter just about falls over at some point—likely in danger of eliciting a few chuckles from human watchers nearby. The problem with leg-lifters is that they often decide they need to mark your furniture, your other pets, and your leg—their own special brand of claiming you as their own. These are hard habits to break, but before you blame your male for peeing on your other dog's head, it could be the other dog's fault. Really. Dogs have a tendency to start smelling where one dog is still peeing and to stick their nose in the stream without thinking.

But curing a dog from lifting his leg in the house is a huge challenge. The best cure is neutering him, and the sooner the better, before he's established the habit. But even that doesn't always help. If he has a favorite indoor spot, try putting his food or water bowl there. That sometimes works. And if all else fails, consider using a belly band, a sort of male diaper for dogs that goes around his midsection and holds an absorbent pad in a strategic place. Once the adult diaper business gets wind of this, it's going to make a fortune. 🐾

Can female dogs cock their legs?

YOU'VE SEEN MALE DOGS COCK THEIR LEGS, but can females do it? The answer is yes.

Female dogs, especially intact or particularly dominant ones, will often lift a leg while they pee. No, not usually as high as a male dog will lift his, but high enough to notice. They do this as an assertion of their confidence and also to mark their territory. You go, girl! 🐾

Why do dogs lick people?

NOTHING SAYS "I LOVE YOU" LIKE DOG SLURPS ON YOUR FACE. Well, sort of. You might not think that if you knew the origin of that behavior. It's a behavior that comes from the natural behavior of wild canid puppies during weaning. Going from nursing at mom's milk bar to crunching down bones is a big step. There's also the problem of getting the food to the pups without dragging it a mile. So mom has a solution: She gorges on whatever food she can, comes back to the pups, and regurgitates the chewed food for them. Other pack members can even help. The pups now see her mouth as the food fountain, and they jump up and lick at it when she returns. This licking is what provokes her to regurgitate (I know some people who feel just like that when dogs lick them in the mouth). The behavior persists, and young puppies lick at any dominant dog (or person's) mouth. Since dogs are mostly cases of arrested development, they often keep up this juvenile behavior throughout life.

Many domestic dogs will still regurgitate for their puppies. Caroline had one dog (Sissy, who was a Best in Show winner) that had to be kept away from her puppies after she ate. Sissy insisted on sharing her warmed and puréed dinner with them, even when they were six months old.

So the next time your dog kisses you on the mouth, you might start wondering if he has ulterior motives—especially if you had steak for dinner. 🐾

Why do dogs jump up on people?

YOUR DOG WAS BORN WITH FOUR LEGS. Then why does he insist on pretending he has only two, pogo-ing up and down, and jumping up on you whenever you come home? You don't do that to him.

That's because you don't have to. In common dog-greeting behavior, dogs are supposed to lick their superior under the chin and around the lips to show their submissiveness. The problem is, our faces are "way up there" to our dogs and practically out of reach. Our dogs jump on us, when they haven't been taught better manners, in order to greet us properly. Since you don't get down on all fours to greet them, they have to do the next best thing and get up on all twos to greet you. 🐾

Is rolling a dog over on its back a good way to show him who's alpha?

YOU MAY HAVE SEEN IT IN SOME BOOKS and on some TV shows: a trainer recommending to roll a dog on his back to show him who's boss. It's a showy stunt and one that seems to intimidate the dog. But should you do it?

In a word, no. There are several reasons for this, but the main reason is, you're likely to get bit and more likely to ruin your relationship with your dog. (Biting alone would certainly ruin your relationship, anyway.) Most dogs react badly to this treatment, called *alpha rolling*, either going completely submissive, freaking out, or becoming more aggressive.

Back in the 1970s and 1980s, dog trainers took a look at wolf behavior and determined that dogs understood what it means to get rolled over when being challenged. What they failed to note was that, in most cases, the submissive wolf was rolling over on his own, not being forced over by the dominant wolf. In fact, the only thing rolling your dog over tells him is that you're the biggest bully on the block and he'd better avoid you. It tells your dog you're really pissed off and you're going to open up a can of whup-ass. It can scare an already frightened dog to the point of biting you in self-defense, and can make an already dominant dog bite you to put you in your place.

Modern trainers don't worry about "showing the dog who's boss" because consistent training will establish that you're boss anyway. Gentle training is more likely to teach the dog to look up to you, and, as it turns out, is the way most alpha wolves lead.

So unless you really intend to have a neurotic and freaked-out dog (and maybe a few stitches), it's better to skip the alpha roll and choose something more enjoyable, like a cinnamon roll. 🐾

Are yawns contagious to dogs?

ABSOLUTELY! Try it sometime while your dog is looking. Yawn at your dog and watch him yawn. Something psychological about watching someone yawn causes us to yawn, be it human or dog.

Yawning is contagious to dogs, just as it is to people. Of course, you just might be boring, and your dog is trying to tell you something. 🐾

Why do dogs smell other dogs' butts?

YOUR DOG MEETS A NEW DOG ON A WALK, and what's the first thing he does? He kind of sidles around to it and tries for a butt sniff while the other dog does the same. And why shouldn't he? The area around the anus has glands that secrete all sorts of personal information about him, maybe about his sexual status, perhaps even about his social dominance—we don't know exactly what. All we do know is that it's the canine equivalent of checking out a fellow conventioneer's badge that says, "Hi, I'm Bowser." 🐾

Why do dogs sniff poop or pee?

HERE'S WHAT I DON'T GET: If dogs have such an acute sense of smell, why must they burrow their noses right into a pile of dog doo-doo in order to get a good whiff, when I can smell it from five feet away? Dog doo-doo is a potpourri of scents that together act like a calling card to other dogs. The feces pick up scents from the glands surrounding the anus, and are coated with pungent anal sac material, which likely is also individualized in scent. They also carry clues about what he had for supper last night.

Urine is an even more important calling card for dogs. It contains information about what sex the dog is, whether it's sexually mature, and, if she's a female, whether she's looking for a beau. Some of this information can be gleaned from sniffing, but the sexual readiness information appears to be best appreciated when tasted, or at least, taken into the mouth and forced into the vomeronasal organ. That's a special organ located between the roof of the mouth and the tip of the nose that is used expressly for analyzing urine samples for sexual-readiness information. OK, so that explains why they have to get so close to check out urine. But as for dog doo-doo? I think they just like to gross us out. 🐾

Why do some dogs eat doo-doo?

FEW THINGS CAN SEND YOU SCRAMBLING for the mouthwash faster than letting your dog plant a big kiss on your lips only to discover he must have been the inspiration for the saying, "sh*t-eating grin." There's nothing worse than a dog that's eaten a turd sandwich.

Experts used to think that dogs dined on doo-doo because of some sort of nutritional deficiency. But studies have shown that poop-partakers include eaters of premium dog foods. So then the theory was that these high-nutrition foods left so much good stuff undigested that the dogs figured it deserved a second chance. After all, one good turd deserves another... Except plenty of turd-tasters eat generic food. The truth is, nobody has found a link between nutrition and *coprophagy* (that's the official name for the practice).

Boredom often gets the blame, but how bored do you have to be? Besides, many dogs that get plenty of activity and attention can't wait to quit their games and go eat poop. Some people claim that not cleaning up the yard causes poop-eating, and while that may be true for some, we've seen dogs race after other dogs that are pooping, in order to eat hot and steamy poop fresh from the doggy dispenser.

So what's the straight scoop on eating poop? Caroline thinks it's a poop deficiency in their diet. But seriously, poop-eaters tend to eat poop because they like it. A few of my dogs won't eat poop unless it's frozen, but once one starts, they all start doing it. More or less, dogs eat poop because they like doing that.

Yum! You were going to eat lunch, weren't you? 🐾

Why do dogs eat plants, dirt, wool, and other weird stuff?

I THOUGHT THEY WERE SUPPOSED to be fang-wielding carnivores! So why do my dogs feast on grass and leaves? In fact, dogs are technically omnivores (although mostly carnivores), which means they eat a variety of foods, including plants and animals. Nobody knows for sure, but biologists point out that when wild canids, like wolves and foxes, eat dead plant-eaters, they also eat the plants in that animal's digestive system. Many wild canids also eat berries as part of their diet. So it could be that it's just natural for your dog to eat his veggies.

Some dogs vomit after eating grass, leading many people to think they eat grass in order to vomit. It does seem that some dogs are more likely to eat it when they have an upset stomach, so there may be something to that. But don't assume your dog to be sick if he's eating grass; some dogs just like it!

Grass and leaves seem OK, but what about dogs that take the suggestion to "eat dirt" too literally? Some dogs dig into the soil, seem to investigate carefully, and happily munch down a mouthful of dirt. Because this habit is sometimes seen in sick dogs in which their illness affects their diet, it's possible that dirt-eating may at times result from a lack of specific minerals in the diet or body. But many perfectly healthy dogs on balanced diets also seem to relish dirt. Maybe they just have a deficiency of dirt in their diet.

Next come the rock-eaters. For unknown reasons, some dogs chew on and swallow rocks. This is a potentially dangerous practice, since they can cause an intestinal blockage and need surgery to save their lives. Nobody knows why they do it, although it's been Maggie's observation that it stems from a habit developed either from boredom or while teething, but so far, the best advice is simply to keep rocks out of their reach.

The compulsion to eat rocks, socks, underwear, coins, and other nonfood objects is known as *pica*, and it's a problem in many species, including dogs and humans. Socks also seem to be a favorite thing for some dogs to eat, and these victuals are very dangerous because they can get into the intestines lengthwise, get stuck, and cause the intestine to accordion in on itself. That requires surgery to fix, or the dog can die. Sometimes drugs to treat compulsive behaviors can help alleviate pica. Meanwhile, pick up your socks!

Why do dogs bury bones?

YOU'VE CLEANED YOUR HOUSE in preparation for your in-laws' visit. Your guest sits on the sofa, gets a funny look on her face, reaches behind her, and pulls a dog bone out from behind the cushion. Something tells you that you've failed inspection. Thanks, Fido.

At least he didn't dig a hole in the sofa to put the bone in. It's happened, plenty of times. Dogs naturally bury food they don't want to eat now in order to save it for later. Dogs with outdoor access may dig a small hole, drop the goods in, and cover it back up by nudging the dirt over it with their nose. Indoor dogs may look for scatter rugs, piles of clothing, or pillows under which to hide their stash. They have a very good memory for where they put things—usually.

Caroline's dogs—picky salukis, the anorexics of the dog world—show their dissatisfaction when they don't like what's being served for dinner by trying to nudge scatter rugs over their food bowls. At least it's better than just walking away from it, which is what they do when they *really* hate what's for supper. They eventually give up when she moves the bowl to a bare tile area, where their noses just make a squeaky sound against the floor. Everybody has to be a food critic. At least she's learned to check under the sofa cushions before company comes. 🐾

Why do dogs rub on disgusting stuff?

EWW, THAT STENCH! If you've ever had to ride back from a walk in the woods in the dead of winter with all your windows wide open and your head hanging out so far you'd make any dog proud, you know what we mean.

What makes the stinky stuff so nasty are chemicals called *thiols*, which are emitted by decomposing animals, poop, and even skunk spray. The smell is particularly strong and pretty vile, which makes us wonder why dogs, with their exquisitely sensitive sense of smell, would feel it necessary to get so up-close-and-personal with it.

Why, oh why, do they do it? Many dog experts think that it's a way for wild canids to cover their scent. After all, you don't have a chance to identify him if you're gagging. Although if the idea is that they can now sneak up undetected on their prey, it strikes us that the bunny is not going to just sit there and think, "Oh, nothing to worry about, just a sixty-pound mound of dead animal headed my way." Or maybe it's a way to let the pack know what disgustingly yummy dinner awaits at the buffet. So then why do dogs roll in dung? Maybe it's to get rid of another odor? Regardless, they sure seem to time it so they do their best rolling right after a bath, with that horrid shampoo smell still on them. Our best guess? Sometimes dogs just gotta be dogs. 🐾

Why do dogs scoot on their butts?

THE FIRST TIME YOU SEE YOUR DOG doing the butt-scooting boogie, it might seem kind of funny, but he's probably not doing it for laughs. Chances are he's scratching his butt, and while, like some old men we know, this may just be an idle pastime reserved for impressing special guests, in most dogs there's a medical reason. One such reason is the possibility his butt really does itch because it has squiggly tapeworm segments gyrating around on it. You can often see the same sort of segments on his fresh stool, or even see dried segments, which look like grains of rice, stuck to the fur around his butt.

If he doesn't have worms, he may have impacted anal sacs. Anal sacs are normally filled with a thick, smelly substance that gets squeezed out along with the feces. In some dogs, the substance gets too thick to fit out of the little anal sac opening, and it builds up inside the sac until the sac gets distended and starts to hurt. The dog rubs his butt along the ground in an effort to relieve the pressure, but it seldom helps much. He needs a visit to the vet, not to the dance studio.

Why do dogs cock their head?

WELL, FOR ONE THING, it looks really cute. Maybe some have even learned that their owners can't say no when they cock their head from one side to another, as if to say, "Did you really say what I thought you did? And by the way, aren't I cute?"

But the truth is that dogs cock their heads when they hear something interesting. They seldom do so in response to seeing something, and never to smelling something, no matter how fascinating. So we can surmise that head cocking probably helps them with some aspect of the auditory signal, most likely in locating its exact source.

In drop-eared dogs, it also lets the earflap of one side fall away from the ear opening, so the sound waves aren't blocked. But neither of these functions really explains why they cock their head when they can plainly hear what you're saying, and plainly see the words coming out of your mouth. Perhaps it really is a way of communicating interest. Maybe it's part of the doggy manual that teaches them to be good listeners. I wish I knew more people who could at least pretend to listen with such rapt fascination. Maybe I should start cocking my head when I want to make sure I get what I want. 🐾

Why do dogs wag their tail?

EVERYBODY KNOWS THAT A wagging tail means a friendly dog, right? Believing that is a good way to get a chunk taken out of your arm. Dogs use their tails to express themselves in many ways, and their wags can mean many different things. Think of a wag like a smile; we all have different sorts of smiles, and they mean all sorts of different things—not always good. A tail that is wagging but tucked indicates submission. A tail that is wagging quickly and broadly can indicate submission or pleasure. A tail wagging slowly but broadly indicates relaxation, playfulness, or anticipation. A tail held high, wagging stiffly in a small arc, indicates dominance or aggressive intention. Overall, a wagging tail indicates a willingness to interact. Reading more into it, especially with a strange dog, may mean misinterpreting it.

But why do they wag their tails at all? Wolves also wag their tails in much the same context. Some biologists believe a wagging tail is a means of distributing scent from the anal region, making hellos easier from a distance. Which is why the only thing worse than a gassy dog is a waggy-tailed gassy dog. 🐾

Do dogs with docked tails miss them?

THE SHORT (GET IT?) ANSWER IS, NO. Most dogs with docked tails have had them docked within a few days of birth. At that early age, the lack of stimulation makes the areas of the brain associated with the missing tail shrink and take on duties devoted to other parts of the body. The few dogs that have their tails docked as adults, perhaps because of repeated injuries or an accident, don't appear to miss them. They wag whatever they have left, and seem unperturbed. It's possible they could suffer from phantom limb sensations, including phantom pain, but if so, they don't make it obvious. Then again, dogs with amputated limbs seem to adjust far more quickly than people do, almost as if they don't even wonder what happened. Then again, what can they say?

Why do dogs turn in a circle before they lie down?

YOU'RE READY TO RELAX IN THE BED WITH YOUR DOG, so you plop down, and your dog hops up beside you, then turns around. And around, and around, and around, until you finally yell, "Lie down already!" Are they trying to see how long it takes you to lose your cool?

Sometimes it seems like it, but they're just doing what comes naturally. Maggie has even had a dog that would walk circles around a coffee table before settling down. The purpose is simple: The dog's wild ancestors circled around and around to stomp the grass good and flat so they had a nice, cozy nest to lie down on.

Somewhere in the evolutionary past, canines that squashed grass flat exceeded the ones that just laid down without squashing it. The grass probably provided a bit more insulation to the ground, and thus an edge to those dogs that did the squashing. Or maybe it just cropped up and seemed like a good idea. Regardless, circling around makes a nice cozy bed outside. Even if it's inside. Until you throw your companion off the bed. 🐾

Why do dogs howl with sirens?

"IT GETS IN THEIR EARS," was the scientific answer my neighbor volunteered. A lot of people think the sirens hurt the dogs' ears, and that's why they howl. But if so, the dogs make no effort to get away from the noise; in fact, all you have to do is look at them and you can see they seem to be enjoying themselves. Instead, it's probably a throwback to their days as pack wolves. Both wolves and dogs howl to keep their packs together, often communicating their whereabouts across great distances. The sound of a siren, or even of an owner's horrible singing, probably mimics some part of howling, enough to elicit your dog's urge to join in. 🐾

Why are some dogs afraid of thunder?

YOU RUSH HOME OUT OF THE RAIN, ready for your dog to greet you. Instead, you're greeted by a drooling, panting maniac who has managed to pee all over the floor and rip your curtains to shreds. The fear can be so intense that dogs might rip their way out of the house and just run blindly. It may start with fear of thunder, but with time extend to firecrackers, slamming doors, the sound of rain, or light flashes. What would cause a normally brave dog to be scared out of his wits?

Many dogs, especially older dogs, are fearful of loud noises, especially thunder. Why? Some people believe their owners act afraid, or coddle the dogs when they act just a little bit scared, and so reinforce that behavior. However, this theory doesn't make sense when several dogs belong to the same person, and often only one is afraid of thunder.

Another idea is that dogs associate a thunder clap with something bad that once happened at the same time. The chances of all these dogs having had a traumatic life experience is pretty low, though. Unless that bad experience is directly related to thunder. Some researchers believe that dogs are more susceptible to static electrical shocks during storms because of their fur. Because many dogs hide in bathrooms, particularly bathtubs, during storms, the story goes that they are automatically seeking to discharge the static electricity built up in the fur, and they do so by being in proximity to metal pipes and other grounds, such as water. No real evidence exists for this idea, though, and it doesn't explain why there aren't just as many furry thunder-phobic cats (although they do exist).

It could just be that dogs are genetically predisposed to fear sudden loud noises. Some families of dogs are more susceptible than others, and young puppies, especially from these susceptible families, naturally jump and act stressed out by such noises.

No matter what the cause, the sooner it's treated, the better the hope for recovery. Treatment involves gradual desensitization, often combined with calming drugs. No, the drugs are for the dog, not you! 🐾

Can dogs have mental illness?

ANY DOG OWNER KNOWS THAT THE ANSWER to this is an unqualified yes without having to consult an expert. Dogs are just plain crazy. But canine behavior experts insist on narrowing down the criteria a tad more when trying to decide whether dogs can really suffer from mental illness.

Many definitions for mental illness exist for humans. They usually refer to alterations in thought, mood, or behavior associated with distress or impaired functioning. It's impossible to tell what dogs are thinking, but some dogs definitely act in ways that cause impaired functioning. Scientists have produced neurosis in dogs by repeatedly presenting them with contradictory information, not too unlike what the typical dog is confronted with at home with his family's sometimes misguided attempts to teach him. Maybe all dogs really are crazy to the extent to which their owners are.

Part of the fun of having a dog is living with a creature that can act crazy and get away with it. Actually, that's probably part of the fun of being a dog! Maybe they're not so crazy after all. 🐾

Can dogs be born bad?

OWNERS OF DOGS WITH SEVERE BEHAVIOR PROBLEMS, including aggression, often naturally blame themselves. They've read all the literature about socialization, and like parents lament, "Where did I go wrong?"

But the truth is, bad dogs can happen to good people. Sometimes dogs are indeed mentally ill and can be treated only with the help of the same drugs used for people with certain problems. We all know of many good-natured dogs that were brought up in the most horrendous and cruel conditions, and of many bad-natured dogs that had every advantage when it came to a loving home and proper socialization. In fact, behaviorists report that the very worst cases of aggression seem to occur independently of how the dog was raised. These dogs may have brain anomalies or chemical imbalances, or like many mentally ill people or sociopaths, may be that way for reasons we don't yet understand. 🐾

Can dogs be obsessive compulsive?

OBSESSIONS REFER TO INTRUSIVE THOUGHTS, and since we can't know what our dogs are thinking, we can't say they have obsessive disorders. A compulsion is a behavior you feel you have to do, even when it interferes with your normal life. These behaviors may be repetitive, exaggerated, sustained, or so intense that they are difficult to interrupt. Obsessive-compulsive people are usually characterized by excessive hand-washing or housecleaning. No such luck with dogs. Dogs also have compulsive disorders, but they never involve cleaning. In dogs, such disorders most often take the form of self-licking, spinning, shadow-chasing, spot-staring, or snapping at imaginary flies.

In some cases, the behavior is fairly mild and doesn't affect the dog's health. In others, the dog licks holes in his own skin, or runs himself to exhaustion, or can't pull himself away in order to eat. Certain breeds, most notably Bull Terriers and some other Terriers, seem predisposed to these compulsive behaviors. Jack Russell Terriers have been known to develop such a compulsion to chase the spots from laser light toys that they spend every waking moment searching for the elusive spot, even when the device was turned off days ago.

In predisposed breeds, care should be taken never to encourage any behavior that could become compulsive. Extra mental and physical exercise may help keep his mind on other things. Once a compulsion develops, he may need drug therapy in order to get over it.

One compulsion that seems universal among dogs is the one to vacuum up every edible morsel in sight. And no drug therapy seems to help that. 🐾

Why do dogs chase their tails?

IF YOU'RE KEEPING UP WITH A PUPPY, you probably feel like you're chasing your tail sometimes. So maybe that's how you make them feel, too, with all this Sit, Stay, and Don't-pee-on-the-floor nonsense. OK, OK, maybe not. The truth is that some dogs, usually older puppies, chase their tail occasionally simply because they can. It's something fun to chase, so they give it a few whirls and either catch it or fall over in a dizzy heap, and go on about their business.

Unfortunately, a few dogs don't stop there. For some dogs, most often bull terriers, followed by German Shepherds, that tail sits there behind them, following them around, taunting them, and they can't help it, they have to go after it! It's funny at first, and some owners may encourage it to entertain guests. But after a while it's not so funny when the tail-chasing becomes compulsive. Apparently, some dogs have a genetic predisposition to compulsively chase their own tail, preferring to do so over eating or playing. It's possible that some stressful event, probably occurring between five and twelve months of age, sets off dogs so predisposed, and off they go in a tail-chasing frenzy. Such dogs may need treatment for compulsive behavior disorder to stop the insanity.

Of course, some tail chasers are simply bored. They may have found a way to both exercise themselves and engage in a little game. Mental and physical stimulation is the best cure for such dogs. In a few cases, itching or pain of the tail or hindquarters may play a part in provoking it.

Then again, maybe it's just because one good turn deserves another. 🐾

Why do dogs like to hang their head out of car windows?

WHO WOULDN'T LIKE TO HANG THEIR HEAD out of the car window? Isn't that the whole idea behind convertibles? Well, that, and looking good. But who can resist the invigorating feel of wind in your hair and bugs in your teeth?

We know better, of course. We know about rocks and road debris and stinging insects and all sorts things that could blind or disfigure us, not to mention muss our hair. But our dogs don't. That's why it's up to us to put the nix on this ultimate auto-eroticism. Spoil sport. 🐾

Can dogs get amnesia?

HOW WOULD YOU TELL THE DIFFERENCE? Maybe he suddenly wouldn't respond to his name or sit when you told him? Like I said, how would you tell the difference?

When people have a severe accident, especially one leading to loss of consciousness, they often get what's called *retrograde amnesia*. That means they may lose their memory of events leading up to their loss of consciousness, perhaps those of only the last few minutes, but sometimes those of the previous week. But it's not like it is in the soaps, where they forget who they are and end up joining the Mob. It's quite possible that dogs suffer from a similar loss of memory regarding events that occurred right before a serious accident, but there's no way for us to know that. On the other hand, maybe that's why some dogs that survive after getting hit by cars wander out in front of the next one as soon as they get off their crutches. 🐾

Can dogs have narcolepsy?

GIVE SKEETER A BONE, take out her leash for a walk, or ask her of she wants to go for a ride, and you get the same response: She keels over and falls fast asleep. She has narcolepsy, a disorder that makes her drop into sleep whenever she gets excited. That's a problem with dogs that have this disorder, because it doesn't take much to get them excited. Even eating, to a dog, is cause for excitement, so Skeeter has to be calmed but physically stimulated so she can stay awake long enough to eat a meal.

Narcolepsy in humans was first described in the late 1800s, but it wasn't until the 1970s that it was identified in dogs. A colony of narcoleptic Dobermans was used to study the disease, and evidence from them, as well as a family of narcoleptic Labradors, demonstrated that the disease is inherited as a recessive trait. The mutated gene is on dog chromosome 12 in Dobermans, but may be at another location in the other fifteen or so breeds susceptible to narcolepsy. The dog research eventually led to the discovery that the same sort of hypocretin deficiency is associated with narcolepsy in both dogs and people.

But if your dog-tired dog keels over, don't just assume she has narcolepsy. She could have heart or neurological problems that need veterinary treatment. Drug therapy can help dogs with narcolepsy, but not always and not completely. Still, this is one case where you shouldn't just let sleeping dogs lie. 🐾

Can dogs be hypnotized?

"YOU ARE GETTING SLEEPY... when I snap my fingers, you will act like a dog...." Well, that might work. But as for getting him to come when called—that remains to be seen.

Claims of animal hypnosis have been around a long time, but what was usually called hypnosis is more often now referred to as *tonic recumbency*. If an animal is restrained in an unnatural position, it will seem to stiffen up and stay there, sort of like what alligator wrestlers do when they "hypnotize" gators. But these are really cases of cataplexy, a sort of frozen state, rather than a suggestive state. Chickens are the best-known example, but I have not been able to find any documented cases of canine tonic recumbency or of canine hypnosis. If somebody could reliably hypnotize dogs and get them to follow posthypnotic suggestions such as don't pee on the floor, don't you think there'd be a line of distraught owners, with their delinquent dogs, shoving money at them? 🐾

Why do some dogs go into a trance when they walk under leaves?

IF YOU'VE NEVER SEEN IT, you won't have any idea what I'm talking about. It's called *trancing*, and it refers to the behavior exhibited when a dog creeps under hanging objects, such as leaves or clothes in a closet, and walks in ultraslow motion beneath them, so they just lightly brush his back; then he turns and does it again and again. During that time he appears almost as though he's in a trance. His eyes seem to glaze over, and he doesn't respond to commands as he normally would. If you touch him or otherwise distract him, he appears irritated but will snap out of it and trot away as if nothing has happened. It's not a seizure, as some people have thought, but a harmless behavior some dogs seem to enjoy. It's reported most often in Bull Terriers and Greyhounds, but has been seen in several other breeds, including Jack Russell Terriers and Basset Hounds. A survey of trancing bull terriers found no relationship between trancing and current or later neurological or behavioral problems.

Caroline has had a couple of Salukis that trance. Her current trancer, Omen, does it about once a day. Hey, it's a cheap high! 🐾

Can dogs become comatose?

SOMEONE WHO IS COMATOSE is in a state of deep and usually prolonged unconsciousness. Even when prompted, comatose people do not awaken or respond to anything around them. Hmmm... sounds like some dogs I know.

Humans may remain comatose for years, kept alive through artificial means. Dogs can also become comatose, from poisoning, low blood sugar, or brain injury. They can be kept alive using the same means that keep comatose humans alive. However, owners seldom elect to do so because of the expense involved and, after a week or so, the low probability that the dog will emerge and be able to function normally. 🐾

Do dogs like to be hugged?

HAVE YOU EVER LOOKED AT YOUR DOG'S FACE when you're hugging him? He looks like a kid who's being hugged by his grandma who has bad breath while all his friends watch and laugh. Humans naturally hug as a sign of affection and comfort. It's natural to us, as our primate ancestors carry their young that way, and the young feel secure when they're being held tightly in their mother's arms.

Dogs don't carry their young in their arms. In fact, the only times dogs naturally feel arms around them is when being bred by another dog, or dominated by another dog. They have no instinctive reason to associate being held with being loved, and they don't naturally enjoy being hugged. Fortunately, dogs are very adaptable, and they learn to close their eyes and make the best of our embarrassing attempts to shower love on them. 🐾

Why do dogs go crazy after a bath?

HAVE YOU EVER GIVEN YOUR DOG A BATH, while he stands there miserably waiting for you to towel him off, and then you step back to admire your squeaky-clean masterpiece only to have him take off, sliding on the floors or rolling around in the dirt like a mad dog? What's with that? When you get out of a bath, *you* don't go insane.

It's probably the simple physics of emotions: For every action, there is an opposite and comparable reaction. The more your dog dislikes the bath, the more he is likely to feel relieved and celebrate once it's over. In fact, it was the observation of his own dog after a bath that led the originator of what became known as the *opponent process theory of emotion* to first come up with his theory.

Another possibility is that your dog doesn't really smell like himself. Instead, he smells like that poo-poo shampoo you bought, and he's trying to get himself to smell more like himself again. Yes, stinky. 🐾

How do dogs know it's time for dinner?

DOGS CAN'T LOOK AT THE CLOCK, but they have an uncanny ability for harassing you if you're just a few minutes late serving their supper. Oh, who am I kidding? They'll try to convince you it's suppertime twenty-four hours a day. But truly, they do know when it's time to eat, and it's not just that they're hungry because they haven't been fed yet.

All animals, including people, seem to have a gut feeling—literally—for when it's time to eat. The gut actually begins to contract and gets ready to rumble right before the time it's used to getting food, and does so regardless of whether the dog had a big or little meal previously. Just as we, and dogs, have a circadian rhythm that controls the sleep-wake cycle, we also have a gut rhythm that tells us it's time—or past time—to eat. Of course, for most dogs, that rhythm seems to be pretty much going full blast all day long. 🐾

How do dogs know it's time for a walk?

YOU'RE SNEAKY. You hide the leash and walking shoes, and just as you're ready to put the shoes on, your dog is at the door, dancing to go for a walk. How did he know?

Well, there are several reasons why dogs know it's time for a walk. First of all, you're not as sneaky as you thought. Dogs are masters of observation, and when they hear you open the closet, put your shoes on, or even sneak toward the door, they know exactly what you're doing. He'll be there with tail wagging and a look on his face saying, "You almost forgot me! But don't worry, I'm here!"

The second way a dog knows it's time for a walk is the timing. If you walk your dog every day at around the same time, I guarantee you that after two walks in a row at about the same time, he'll be waiting impatiently for you on the third day. Dogs do know time and have an internal chronometer, just like people do. That's why switching to daylight savings time or back to standard time throws dogs off as much as it throws us off.

So the time, combined with your dog's observations, tell him when he's going for a walk—and why it seems nothing short of telepathy, when it's not. So don't fight it—just take him for the walk! 🐾

Why do dogs like balls?

YOU'VE SEEN THEM. Whether it's a Labrador Retriever or a tiny Yorkshire Terrier, there's a dog with a ball in his mouth. In fact, we did an unofficial survey and 8 out of 10 dogs liked balls. (The holdouts were Maggie's Alaskan Malamutes, who wouldn't dare touch one of those things.)

In all seriousness, why do dogs like balls? Well, first of all, dogs are predators and, as predators, they have a built-in instinct to chase after things that move. In their domestication, the hunting aspect has been watered down, and because of this, chasing (rather than killing) became fun. Balls are handy objects that roll easily (you don't see cubes rolling around do you?) and balls that are about the size of a tennis ball fit handily in a dog's mouth.

So, the ball's shape and size are just conducive to fun. Besides, who doesn't like a big, slobbery, slimy tennis ball? 🐾

2

CANINE
INTELLIGENCE

Do dogs think?

DESPITE WHAT SOME OF THEIR wilder behavior might suggest, dogs do think. At least, we think they do. Then again, how can you prove that anyone, other than yourself, really thinks?

Scientists have come up with a few theories and tests that have bearing on the subject. One requirement of conscious thinking is that you be aware not just of what is in front of you at the moment, but also a mental representation of items that are out of your sensory range. And one way this is tested is by looking for something called *object permanence*. If a cookie is placed before you, and then a sheet of paper blocks your view of the cookie, you don't think the cookie has suddenly disappeared from the earth. But babies do, up until they're about eight or nine months old.

You don't need a laboratory test to tell you that dogs, like us, have object permanence. We close the cupboard with the dog cookie box inside, but they're not fooled. A hunter shoots two ducks, and they fall into tall grass. His dog doesn't for a second think they've disintegrated. He remembers where they both fell and brings them back. Laboratory tests have shown that puppies conceive of object permanence to some degree by five weeks of age, and show it reliably by eight weeks. Even when the test is made more difficult, by first hiding the object in a container and moving the container, and using up to five locations at the same time, adult dogs still pass the test, demonstrating that they have some sort of abstract mental representation of objects and their environment.

Another component of conscious thought involves the ability to see from another individual's point of view. Young children can't do this, but dogs can. For example, if you leave your baked chicken on the table, your dog may look at it longingly, but he probably won't try to snatch it right in front of you. But if you leave the room, or in some cases, turn your back, he seems to know that you can't see him, and what you don't know can't hurt him, so he snatches it. Scientists actually performed a similar experiment under controlled conditions, and found this to be true. They placed some food on the floor and forbade the dog to eat it. Then they either looked at the dog, left the room, turned their back, or shut their eyes. When the people were looking, dogs took longer before they approached the food, and when they did approach it, they did so in a more roundabout way. But when the people weren't looking, they tended to go right up to the food. These results are consistent with the idea that dogs can comprehend your state of attention.

Dogs also seem to use this awareness of others' perceptions in order to deceive others. They may hide stolen treats from other dogs, or bark at imaginary threats so the other dog will desert its treat, while the original barker rushes back in to claim it. They regularly use deceit as part of their play behavior, egging you on to grab for the toy they hold tantalizingly just out of reach, pretending that you actually have a chance.

Laboratory tests may suggest that dogs think, but nobody who lives with a dog could imagine why such tests would even be necessary. It's not just wishful thinking.

Do dogs with little heads have little brains and little minds?

DON'T SAY THAT AROUND ANY CHIHUAHUAS! You'll have trouble, my friend.

Head size doesn't correlate with intelligence for several reasons. For one, brain size in dogs doesn't vary as much as head size. In a tiny-headed dog, the brain takes up most of the back skull, with very thin bone protecting it. In large-headed dogs, the brain is larger, but not proportionally. The bone of the skull is much thicker in these dogs, with the comparatively small brain nestled deep within.

Next, brain size naturally increases with body size, or more accurately, as a function of body surface area. That's because much of the brain is devoted to sensing and controlling the body, and the bigger the body, the more brain is needed to represent each part. It's true that some species have a larger brain than you'd expect for their body surface area, and some less, and scientists often do use this "encephalization quotient" as an estimate of intelligence.

Nobody has compared the encephalization quotient in various sizes or breeds of dogs, however, and even if they did, what would it show? We haven't been able to come up with fair tests of intelligence between species, or even between breeds. So suffice it to say that any dog that has convinced a human to wait on him and care for him in exchange for a few tongue licks and tail wags is one smart pup. 🐾

Is there such a thing as phrenology for dogs?

PHRENOLOGY WAS BASED on the idea that as certain parts of the brain became more developed, they would cause bumps in the overlying area of the skull. Thus, by carefully feeling somebody's skull, a trained phrenologist could determine all sorts of things about their intellectual and emotional propensities. The only problem with the theory is that it didn't work, at least not for humans. For one thing, we still don't know enough about the brain to pinpoint where the "life of the party" center is in humans, or where the "catch that ball" center is in dogs. For a second thing, even if we did know where such centers existed, the skull simply doesn't conform to the brain's shape like that. It has bumps, sure, but they don't reflect underlying bulges in the brain. So just because a dog has a narrow head doesn't mean he's narrow-minded. 🐾

Do dogs remember incidents?

THIS IS ONE THAT THE EXPERTS aren't in agreement with, mainly because we can't ask a dog what he remembers. Many experts believe that dogs don't remember specific incidents day to day—but then, people don't seem to remember them either—so it's hard to judge what a dog does remember.

However, it's been Maggie's experience that dogs remember things all the time—probably better than we do. With her own dogs, her Malamutes would recognize areas on the trail where they had hiked—and where they had encountered other animals or stopped for a rest. When her dogs went to places where they had seen other animals (even years before), they would get excited in that area and look around. When they arrived at a place where they had stopped for a rest, they'd start pulling off to the side even before the people did.

Another case in point is Maggie's first dog, Conan. He liked going to the vet—until he got neutered. Then the vet was a source of fear and woe. It's pretty obvious he remembered going in—and leaving minus a few key body parts.

So, from anecdotal evidence, it appears that dogs do remember incidents. And it makes sense. Otherwise, how could we train a dog if the dog couldn't remember what he did the day before? Or how would your dog know that he hated a particular dog that growled at him before? It just makes sense that they remember certain incidents. 🐾

Are some breeds really that dumb?

"I WOULD RATHER TRAIN A STRIPED ZEBRA to balance an Indian club than induce a Dachshund to heed my slightest command." That's what the writer E. B. White had to say. He was apparently a Dachshund owner.

We all have ideas about how easy one breed is to train versus another. When a popular book tallied input from obedience judges to rank breeds from most to least obedient, the breeds ranked as most obedient were no surprise: the Border Collie, Poodle, German Shepherd, Golden Retriever, Doberman Pinscher, Shetland Sheepdog, and Labrador Retriever. Those ranked as least obedient were the Afghan Hound, Basenji, Bulldog, Chow Chow, Borzoi, Blood-hound, and Pekingese. To owners of these breeds, them was fightin' words.

But the ability to follow commands is not necessarily the same thing as being smart. Of the seven most trainable breeds, six come from herding or retrieving backgrounds, jobs for which the ability to follow human cues is important. A good retriever must be able to follow its handler's directions to locate fowl downed out of the dog's sight, or to avoid swimming into danger. A good herder must be able to follow the shepherd's directions to place the sheep where they are wanted. If these breeds don't follow orders, they're history.

Of the bottom seven breeds, four are hunting hounds, breeds in which independent thinking is more critical to success. A hound that continuously looks to its handler for directions is useless.

In addition, of these bottom seven breeds, four (the Afghan Hound, Basenji, Chow Chow, and Pekingese) are considered to be progenitor breeds, according to recent DNA research. That means these breeds share more genes in common with ancestral wolves and perhaps are less affected by the domestication pressures of trainability. Domestication has selected for dogs that have an aptitude for training to some greater degree than do typical wolves, which are notoriously hard to train. Wolves react to forceful obedience training by fleeing and struggling, which are reactions adaptive to their lives in the wild.

People with highly trainable dogs tend to assert that trainability and intelligence go hand in hand; people with less easily trained dogs tend to assert that refusal to follow rote commands is a sign of intelligence. Both are correct. If intelligence is defined as an innate ability to learn or perform at the optimal mental capacity to perform a function, then intelligence in one breed should be defined differently from that in another. An intelligent Border Collie reads and controls sheep; an intelligent Saluki reads and catches jackrabbits. If they switched jobs (or brains), they would be both be labeled dumb.

John Paul Scott and John L. Fuller's landmark study of dog behavior included one of the so-called smartest breeds, the Shetland Sheepdog, and one of the bottom-ranked breeds, the Basenji, along with Wire Fox Terriers, Beagles, and Cocker Spaniels. He raised and tested these dogs under identical conditions, yet they tended to respond to training differently according to breed. During leash training, Basenjis vigorously fought the leash, Shelties repeatedly leapt on and tripped their handlers, and Beagles howled. In a test of how well they could learn to remain still when being weighed, 70 percent of the Cocker Spaniels but only 10 percent of the Fox Terriers could remain still for one minute. In general, for tests involving forced restraint, Cocker Spaniels did best, followed by Shelties. Fox Terriers tended to play-fight when restrained by hand, but did better from a distance. Beagles seemed restless when restrained, and Basenjis attempted to escape.

The tables turned when training went from methods employing force to methods employing rewards. When breeds were compared on their ability to run to a box containing a reward, the Basenjis were the clear stars, with Shelties lagging far behind. The Basenjis and Cocker Spaniels outshined the others when it came to traversing a raised plank to get to food; the Shelties mostly failed the exercise. The Basenjis were also best at a task that required them to use their paws to uncover a dish of food; Cocker Spaniels were worst at this task.

The Shelties were the worst maze runners. When placed in the maze, they tended to become upset and hesitant compared with the other breeds. Basenjis were confident and scored well at first, but then seemed to lose motivation. Fox Terriers tended to try to bite their way out. The results were reminiscent of the famous maze-bright and maze-dull rat lines developed in the 1920s by selectively breeding the best and worst maze-running rats. Later studies showed that the difference did not reflect brightness versus dullness, but boldness versus timidity; the maze-dull rats simply froze in a maze situation. Because of differences in breed-typical reactions and abilities, there's no single test of intelligence that is adequate among the various breeds.

But if you have a dog of a breed not known for trainability, it doesn't mean it can't be trained. In the hands of a gifted trainer, a Peke has earned the obedience world's highest title of Obedience Trial Champion (OTCH). And anybody who saw the Ringling Brothers and Barnum & Bailey Circus troupe of Borzois taught by the famed animal-training family of Gunther Gebel-Williams would have to assume them among the most trainable of breeds, rather than in the bottom seven. Still, if you want an obedient dog, go with the dogs ranked at the top. But if you like challenges—go with the freethinkers. 🐾

Can dogs be mentally deficient?

LET'S FACE IT: Dogs do an assortment of amazingly stupid things. That's one of their appealing qualities. Where else can you find a roommate who can be counted on to make you both laugh and feel smart almost every day? But some dogs do stupider things than others. And while we can't test them on standardized IQ tests to see if they're really suffering from some kind of learning disability, we can rest assured that when it takes six months to teach Einstein to sit, we have a clue.

The truth is, like people, dogs have normal variation in intelligence. Even dogs of the same breed, from the same litter, can have vastly different abilities when it comes to learning. Genetics plays a role, as do early mental stimulation and experiences. Certain chromosomal disorders can lead to slow behavior in dogs, just as trisomy 21 (Down's syndrome, which is caused by an extra chromosome) does in people. A Greyhound breeder had a dog once that she was sure had something akin to Down syndrome. He was sweet, but dumb. Very dumb. She was able to have a *karyotype* (catalog of his chromosomes) done of him and, sure enough, he had an extra chromosome.

Brain injury can also cause mental slowness. Puppies born with hydrocephalus have abnormal pressure on their brain, and while they can survive into adulthood, they almost always have learning deficits for the rest of their lives.

Fortunately, dogs don't have to graduate from college, or even trade school, in order to have a bright future. All they need is you, keeping them on the equivalent of canine welfare. It's a dog's life.

Can dogs count?

HAVE YOU EVER POURED A HANDFUL OF TREATS into a pile, then realized you gave away too many and took some back? She'll never notice, right? Wrong. Dogs can apparently tell when things don't add up. Specifically, if you do like researchers did and show a dog a couple of treats, then hide those treats behind something while your dog sees you add another to the pile, then reveal the whole pile to him once again, he won't be fazed if the treats add up correctly. But if you trick him, for instance by making it look like you're adding one treat but instead adding two, when you reveal the pile the dog will stare at it longer than usual, as if trying to figure out why the count is off. This is the same test researchers give babies (except they don't use dog treats), and at a certain age babies start to stare longer when the amount added doesn't match the amount they see. Scientists say that this is evidence that dogs, and babies, have some inborn mathematical ability, because they realize something is amiss when $1 + 1 = 3$.

Do dogs know calculus?

WHO KNEW YOU HAD A LATENT MATH whiz whizzing at your feet! According to one mathematician, dogs, or at least his dog, know calculus. When he throws a ball in the water at an angle to the shoreline, his dog has several options. He can swim right out after it at an angle, he can run along the shore until he's opposite to it and then plunge in, or he can run partway and then plunge in, so he swims a shorter distance. It turns out that his dog, like many dogs, chooses this last option, which it also turns out is the best strategy you'd come up with if you fed the numbers into a computer and figured out the fastest route to the ball. Now, I wouldn't go so far as to say a dog has a mind like a computer, but he just may instinctively perform some behaviors based on complex math.

If only I'd known. Instead of claiming the dog ate my calculus homework, I could have just had him do it for me. 🐾

Do dogs understand it when you point?

HOW OFTEN HAVE YOU POINTED to something you wanted your dog to see only to have your dog stare at your finger? At least, that's what mine do. But apparently mine are dumb, because in controlled studies researchers have found that dogs can interpret the significance of pointing. When the researchers hid food beneath one of two bowls, and then had people point to the correct bowl, the dogs usually picked the correct bowl (even though steps were taken to prevent them from choosing on the basis of smell). They could even do this when the person just stared at the bowl. Wolves, however, were very poor at this task, suggesting that dogs may have evolved the ability to interpret human signals as a function of living with us. As unpredictable as most people are, this had to be a handy trait to evolve. But don't they know it's not polite to point? 🐾

Can dogs learn to read?

IF YOU'VE EVER HAD A PUPPY, you've probably experienced firsthand the voracious canine hunger for printed matter. The problem, of course, is that we have something else in mind when we speak of devouring a book.

There's actually a book about teaching your dog to read. Unfortunately, my dog didn't read it. In fact, she ate it. So we had to look into the scientific literature, and here's what we found. The earliest "reading dog" on record comes from an 1888 report about a Poodle (we should have known) whose owner taught him to fetch cards bearing such words as "food," "bone," "water," and "out" in response to the person's request. He made some interesting mistakes, such as fetching "door" when he was asked for "food," suggesting that he was keying in on some visual aspect of the word's shape or features.

More recent experiments have shown that so-called reading dogs tend to recognize words based on their overall length or pattern. For example, a dog might be able to reliably choose "cat" versus "canine" but not "cat" versus "dog," suggesting he is making his choice based on the overall length of the words rather than the words themselves. So yes, you can teach dogs to recognize particular words, but don't expect them to pick up a copy of *War and Peace,* or even *Dick and Jane,* and get anything out of it but chewing pleasure. 🐾

Can some foods make dogs smarter?

YOUR GRANDMOTHER MAY HAVE BEEN right when she said fish was brain food.

Certain types of fish contain high levels of omega-3 fatty acids. In a recent study, puppies fed various levels of omega-3 fatty acids were subsequently trained to associate a symbol, either a cube or a sphere, with the correct direction to take in a T-shaped maze. Puppies whose dams were fed diets high in these fatty acids, and which were also fed them after weaning, not only had significantly higher levels of docosahexaenoic acid (DHA), a component of omega-3 fatty acids, in their red blood cell membranes, but also scored significantly better on the maze test than did those reared on the low omega-3 fatty acid diet. Based on these results, puppy foods are now available with DHA added to them.

This same result has been reported in human infants. Children born to mothers who had taken cod liver oil during pregnancy and lactation scored higher on a mental processing test at four years of age compared with children whose mothers had taken corn oil.

Omega-3 fatty acids have even been implicated in reducing criminal behavior. One recent study found that supplementing the diets of poor children in Mauritania with higher-quality food, including fish, which contain omega-3 fatty acids, reduced their criminal activity when they got older. Another recent study found that adding fatty acid supplements to the diets of adult prisoners decreased prison violence.

Understandably, both studies are somewhat controversial, but if giving my dog a fish oil pill will make him come when called and quit peeing on the floor, I'm all for it. 🐾

Do dogs understand the concept of time?

HOW LONG IS THAT IN DOG SECONDS? It's hard to know how our sense of time compares with our dogs', but we do know that you can give them the best watch in the world and they'll scarcely bother to glance at it. But you know your dog has a concept of time; he knows when you usually get up in the morning, so he times his best barking for about a half hour earlier. He knows when you're one minute late serving his supper, so he threatens to hit the speed-dial number to report cruelty to animals. Famous cases of loyal dogs abound, such as Hachiko, the dog who met his owner at the railway station every day at precisely 5:30. His owner died while at work one day, but the dog continued to show up, every day at the same time, for the rest of his life.

But scientific studies of canine time perception are rare. What we do know is that dogs are adept at learning what's called *fixed interval responses*; that is, if you give a dog a task to do, such as pressing a lever, but reward him for it only precisely every half hour (or any other period of time), the dog will quickly figure out the time interval, laze around in between time, and when the time approaches, start frenetically pressing the lever. Sort of like somebody who knows the boss always looks in at a certain time. 🐾

Do dogs get Alzheimer's?

DO YOU HAVE A DOG THAT WALKS into the room and looks confused? Does he bark randomly through the night? Does he forget he's supposed to be housebroken?

You may be thinking Alzheimer's, and you wouldn't be far from the truth. Very old dogs can suffer from a type of senility known as canine cognitive dysfunction syndrome (CDS). With CDS, the dog forgets he's house-trained, or gets stuck behind furniture, or stares into a room as if he's forgotten where he is, or barks for no apparent reason.

This senility is really frustrating for dog owners, but fortunately, there's medication that can help your pet with "doggy Alzheimer's." The current medicine is called Anipryl (selegiline) and is available only through a veterinarian. It doesn't work in all cases, but for those dogs that it does work on, it's like night and day.

3

THE DOG'S EMOTIONS

Do dogs mourn?

IF YOU'VE EVER HAD A LOVED ONE DIE, you know how it feels. It's an empty that you can't ignore. You feel sad and depressed. In other words, you mourn for the loss of that person.

But can dogs feel that sense of loss, and mourn? Do they get depressed when an owner or another dog passes away?

Most definitely. It has been Maggie's experience that dogs that lose littermates, kennel mates, and pals go through mourning. They will often stop eating, become exceedingly vocal, and look for the other dog. Maggie cites the love story between Panda and Miki, which were cousins Maggie had adopted. Because they were only three years apart and seemed to like each other, they did everything together, including sleeping, eating, and running beside each other on a sled team.

Miki came down with a terrible cancer that was extremely aggressive. After treating it without success, Maggie had to put Miki down. When Maggie came home from the vet's, Panda was looking at her as if upset. She'd cry and whine constantly, looking for Miki. She also stopped eating.

Maggie tried to have another dog stay with her, but Panda didn't care. Eventually, Maggie moved Panda to a new kennel, surrounded by other dogs. The change of venue seemed to make Panda less upset, but time seemed to help her the most.

This is one story out of many, but other dog owners seem to confirm these observations as well. Yes, dogs grieve, just as we do. 🐾

Can you trust someone your dog hates?

YOU'VE HEARD THE OLD ADAGE of never trusting someone your dog dislikes. But if your dog dislikes your new boyfriend or Aunt Edna, should you say goodbye to them? Maybe, or maybe not. It really depends on what your dog doesn't like about them.

Dogs are great observers. Wolves, and subsequently dogs, have developed amazing powers of observation that would rival Sherlock Holmes. They observe things that you and I might never notice: a person's posture, certain reactive smells (such as those of sweating from stress, and possibly other smells associated with emotions), facial expressions, and other things dogs look for when sizing up a person or a situation.

Your dog already has some clues about the emotional state of the person who visits even before he or she says a word. He'll be quick to pick up on whether the person is anxious or fearful—or even if he doesn't like dogs. Your dog reacts according to what he sees and smells. If he doesn't like it, he doesn't like the person.

This works pretty well if you have a bad guy who is intent on doing harm. His body posture, combined with his scent, can be a signal that he is up to no good. However, this scent thing can get a bit out of hand. Let's say your Aunt Edna smokes cigarettes or your boyfriend decides to try some new aftershave to impress you. Your dog may decide he doesn't like the cigarette smell or doesn't like the aftershave, or he may be associating that scent with something threatening.

Or maybe your aunt is just a little too nervous around your dog, and that anxiety is being telegraphed through her body language and scent.

While dogs can be astute judges of character, they can, like others, be occasionally misled. So, just because your dog hates them doesn't mean these people are bad. It may just mean that your boyfriend needs to change his aftershave, not his entire personality.

Do dogs have friends and enemies?

WE ALL KNOW WHAT IT'S LIKE TO HAVE FRIENDS. We also know what it's like to have enemies—or at least, people we don't like. But can dogs have friends and enemies? The answer is—yes.

Dogs are pack animals, which means they feel most secure when they're with their buddies. These buddies are the ones that will back them up and help them hunt, as well as help care for pups as needed. These buddies are either members of their pack or dogs they consider part of their "extended pack."

So, what about enemies? Oh yes, dogs can certainly hate other dogs. Maggie had two female dogs that despised each other so intensely that there was no way they would get along. One would egg the other on to the point where they would get into a fight each time they were together. In the end, keeping them separate was the only way to ensure peace.

Do dogs feel jealousy and spite?

"HE DID THIS TO SPITE ME!" How many times have you heard a pet owner say that when their dog has chewed up a favorite item or peed on the floor? Or maybe there's a new boyfriend or a new baby in the house. You may be thinking that dogs feel jealousy and spite, in spite of themselves.

Spite (which causes people to do something tit-for-tat) is a pretty complex emotion. It requires us to see behavior we don't like and to associate it with doing something so contrary that it will irk the other person. For example, a teenage girl might not like the way her brother teased her the other day and so she hides her brother's backpack to retaliate. That's spite. However, dogs don't think that way.

A dog associates a particular occurrence with what is going on *right now*. For example, if you reward your dog while he's barking, he will continue to bark to get the reward. If you spank your dog for chewed-up shoes (we don't recommend spanking, by the way), your dog is likely to consider the chewed-up shoes as being bad—not the act of chewing up the shoes.

Now let's take it one step further. Your dog chews up your shoes while you're gone. You may think he's "getting back at you" for being gone so long. Actually, what is happening is that your dog is getting anxious and resorts to something that comforts him— something with your scent. He chews it because it feels good. You come home, discover your chewed-up shoes, and get angry. Your dog is left puzzled and dismayed that you came home and punished him. See the problem?

What about jealousy? Dogs can feel as though they aren't getting enough attention, certainly, but they don't associate their rambunctiousness with anger or spite. Instead, they react to the lack of attention by trying to draw your attention toward them, using good or bad means.

So, instead of thinking your dog is doing something to spite you, try to see that your dog may need more attention and training. 🐾

Do dogs fall in love?

WE'VE ALL SEEN THE DISNEY MOVIES where a boy dog meets a girl dog and they fall in love, such as in *Lady and the Tramp*, but do dogs fall head-over-hocks in love with other dogs? And is it really romantic?

We know that dogs do indeed make friends, and many are boyfriend/girlfriend–type relationships. But is it love?

Dogs, unlike wolves, don't mate for life. In fact, if a female dog comes into season (heat), you can guarantee that all the male dogs, regardless of their love for their current canine "girlfriend," will be homing in on the new female. After all, it's instinct and hormones. So, the concept of falling in love goes out the window right there.

However, that doesn't mean that dogs can't feel some affection for one another that goes beyond the physical. Maggie has seen several cases where dogs that lived with each other seemed to bond more closely than with others. In fact, several of her dogs have a preference for certain dogs over others. Caroline adds that, when they're in season, her female dogs show distinct preferences for certain males, snarling at some suitors and flirting with others. Is it love or something else?

Well, sadly, we can't ask a dog if he or she has ever had a heartthrob, so the question is completely debatable. Maggie thinks that dogs can have strong feelings toward other dogs, but whether it is "love" leaves much up to the interpreter. So, the answer is, maybe.

Do dogs cry?

YOU'RE SITTING DOWN ON A Saturday afternoon watching those sappy old movies and bawling your eyes out. Your dog may be watching it along with you, but never sheds a tear. Or maybe he does. Do dogs cry?

Dogs' emotions aren't tied to their tear ducts. While dogs do get teary-eyed, they do so because there is some sort of irritant in their eyes. Some dogs' eyes are naturally teary simply because the ducts that normally drain tears from the eyes are clogged or too small, so the tears have to run out onto the face. Eye infections, malformed eyelids, eyelashes growing inward, foreign bodies, or scratched corneas can all cause the eye to produce excessive tears.

So, if your dog is shedding a tear or two over a movie, it's time for a trip to the veterinarian for an eye exam.

Do dogs have a sense of humor (and can they play practical jokes)?

DOGS ARE CAPABLE OF SOME very complex emotions, but do they have a sense of humor? Well, we didn't have to look far to find the answer—all we had to do was look in Maggie's own house. You see, Maggie owns the clown of the dog world, the Alaskan Malamute.

Both independent and smart, these dogs can come up with tricks all their own. They're really famous in show rings for embarrassing their owners, as Maggie will attest. She's heard of a Malamute bitch that decided to finish her conformation show walking on her hind legs. While a crowd pleaser, Maggie doubted it impressed the judge.

One of her own dogs used to play tricks on her—tricks that Maggie inadvertently taught her. One was a "made you look" kind of game, where you try to trick the other person (in this case, the dog) to look up. You look up really fast and then back at the dog. When the dog looks up, you laugh. (We lead very boring lives, OK?) Maggie's Malamute, Kiana, started instigating that game on her own and fooled Maggie quite a bit. Until one time when Maggie refused to play—and a spider fell on her head!

Many dogs love being the center of attention and understand that laughter is good. So, they become natural hams, because they really do like making people laugh. So when you see a dog doing something funny, you can guess that yes, indeed, they love humor as much as we do. Maybe even more so. 🐾

Do dogs get embarrassed?

IT'S HARD TO IMAGINE an animal that licks his privates as one that might get embarrassed. But oddly enough, dogs appear to become embarrassed when something happens that they didn't intend.

Maggie knows about this one coyote that tried to cross a runway while planes were taking off and landing. The coyote was so busy watching for planes, he ran into a marker light. He shook his head a couple of times, glared at the marker light, and then moved on. He acted as if the whole thing didn't happen.

Now, granted that this was not quite a dog, but a relative of the dog, you can still see where this might go. When unexpected things happen to dogs and it doesn't go as planned, they seem to try to ignore that they ever occurred. You can sort of imagine one whistling innocently in this situation.

Is there actual proof of dogs being embarrassed? Well, embarrassingly enough, they haven't the ability to tell us, so we really don't know. But there's a good chance that they do.

4

THE
CANINE BODY

Do rabid dogs really foam at the mouth?

CUJO SET THE STANDARD for the vision of a drooling, foaming rabid dog, but is this really how a rabid dog looks—and acts? Cujo may have been an overachiever when it came to the rabid urge to kill, but some of what he displayed was accurate. Rabid animals do often drool excessively. But as we'll see later, not as a rule at the same time they're attacking.

The drooling occurs because the virus causes painful spasms of the muscles that control breathing and swallowing, and swallowing eventually becomes so painful that the dog tries not to do so. Just looking at water can even cause painful spasms, which is how the word *hydrophobia* (fear of water) came into being. The infected salivary glands also produce too much saliva, and since it hurts too much to swallow it, the saliva pools in the mouth and eventually drains out as drool or foam. This is complicated by the fact that as the muscles of the jaw become paralyzed, the lower jaw tends to hang open. Pretty, eh?

But just because a dog is foaming at the mouth, don't assume he has rabies (of course, if you don't know him, maybe you should assume it just to be on the safe side). Excessive foaming or drooling can be caused by a foreign object in the mouth, getting a bad-tasting substance in the mouth (even getting too close to some toads will do it), or problems with the throat or tonsils.

But back to Cujo. Do all rabid dogs attack? No. Rabies has three stages. In the first stage, which lasts two to four days, the dog may chew at the bite site, lose his appetite, run a fever, and show some slight behavioral changes. It's the second stage, which lasts two to three days, during which he may exhibit the mad-dog symptoms. He'll become restless, may roam, may lose fear of his natural enemies, and may attack anything, even inanimate objects. Finally, in the third stage, the muscles of the jaw and throat become paralyzed, his lower jaw tends to hang open, and he drools and foams at the mouth. The paralysis spreads to the rest of his body, and he dies. Some dogs skip over the second stage and seem to go directly to the third stage, so not all rabid dogs go mad. And mad dogs usually don't drool, since the two symptoms occur at different stages of the illness.

But if you see a dog foaming at the mouth and biting at anything that moves, don't try to second-guess things. Run away! Or, well, sneak away. And call the authorities. 🐾

Do dogs blush?

BLUSHING IN PEOPLE SEEMS to occur when you feel you've broken some sort of social norm and everybody knows it. Well, here's the problem: Dogs lick their privates in public, they mate on roadsides, and they don't seem to mind it when you blame it on the dog, even when it really is their fault. What social norms? How do you make a creature like that blush?

Dogs don't blush out of embarrassment, but some dogs, notably the Pharaoh hound, do blush out of excitement. An account from the XIXth Egyptian dynasty even describes one of these dogs while hunting: "...his face glows like a god."

Blushing occurs when adrenaline causes the heart rate to increase and blood vessels that deliver blood to the face dilate. More blood than usual flows to the face, and you can see the Pharaoh hound's normally flesh-colored nose and the inside of the ears flush red. But don't try embarrassing them just to see the show. It won't work, and you may end up being the red-faced one instead of the dog, while the onlookers merely think you've lost your mind. 🐾

Do old dogs get gray hair?

IT'S TOUGH GETTING OLD—and one of the first signs is graying hair. Will you have to break out the hair dye to keep your dog feeling good about himself as he ages? Possibly, although some dogs, like some people, don't show gray as well. The dogs with dark-colored hair show gray more readily, starting at the chin and muzzle. Some will show gray on the paws and eventually all over the head.

Just don't show him a mirror.

Can dogs be albinos?

ALBINOS OCCUR IN HUMANS, monkeys, squirrels, snakes, mice, rabbits—in fact, most species. You'd think the way people tend to breed any animal that unusual, especially dogs, you'd see white-furred pink-eyed dogs all over the place. But you don't.

Remember, albino animals aren't just white animals. They have a complete lack of pigment in the fur, skin, eyes, and nose. When was the last time you saw a dog like that? The truth is, albino dogs are rare. Occasional instances do occur, but only in the Doberman pinscher has a line of albinos been developed. These dogs have no pigment except for blue eyes.

OK, here's something for you science geeks: "Classic" albinism is caused by a defect in the "C" series of coat-color alleles so that the enzyme tyrosinase, which is important for producing melanin, isn't produced. Such albinos are called *tyrosinase-negative*. Other (tyrosinase-positive) albinos have normal tyrosinase, and their mutation appears to be at another locus. The few pink-eyed albino dogs, as well as the albino Dobermans, studied so far have been tyrosinase-positive, suggesting their mutation lies at this other locus, designated "P" for now. Whatever mutation is responsible, it appears to be transmitted in a classic recessive fashion. Albino dogs often suffer from vision problems, extreme sensitivity to bright light, sunburn, and skin cancer. Doberman Ppinscher breeders do not advocate breeding or buying albino Dobes for these reasons. And really, with all the bizarre dog traits out there, you can find something a lot more unusual than an albino dog. 🐾

Do dogs get sunburned?

WHO GOES TO THE BEACH with a fur coat on and still gets a sunburn? Your dog, that's who. Or at least some dogs. It's true that a thick coat works just like your clothing to block out the sun's rays. But many dogs have thin fur, at least over certain areas such as their stomach, chest, and muzzle. And like people, some dogs are dark-skinned while others are light-skinned. If you have a dog with a naked light-skinned tummy that likes to lounge around on her back in the sun, she's a candidate for a sunburn. The most common site of sunburn, however, is probably the nose. Not all dogs have black noses, and lighter-colored noses, especially pink ones, are very susceptible to burning and a condition known as *nasal solar dermatitis*. This can be a really bad problem for dogs and can lead to infections. And just like people, sunburns in dogs predispose them to skin cancer.

If your dog is fair-nosed or fair-skinned—or especially, hairless!—and is going to spend time in the sun, you need to put sunscreen on her just as you would on yourself. Only beware: She may lick hers off, so make sure it's nontoxic. Oh well, at least you can tell your friends you rubbed suntan lotion on a topless female at the beach. Just leave out the part about the hairy chest. 🐾

Do some dogs have higher body temperatures than others?

IF YOU TOUCH A HAIRLESS DOG'S SKIN, the first thing you'll notice is that it feels kind of weird—although why naked dog skin should feel weirder than naked person skin is hard to explain. The second thing you'll notice is that he feels hot to the touch! Are hairless dogs really "hot dogs," as many people claim?

Normal body temperature for dogs ranges from 100.5 to 102.5 degrees Fahrenheit (38 to 39.2 degrees Celsius). Smaller dog temperatures tend to be somewhat higher, and larger dogs' lower, within that range. Hairless dogs are no exception. They simply feel hotter because they don't have a layer of fur insulating their skin from yours. But that hot temperature came in handy centuries ago, when laying one across your stomach was a favored way to cure a stomachache—the world's first heating pad!

Does shaving a dog's fur make him cooler?

YOU HEAR IT ALL THE TIME: "Never shave your long-coated dog in the summer. That thick coat insulates your dog from both the cold and the heat." Huh? I don't know about you, but I have never found that wearing my down parka in the summer kept me cool. Why should a dog's coat be different? And consider this: How many wild animals that live around the equator have long coats? Hold on, still counting, yep, that would be—zero! There must be a reason for this, and the reason lies in the laws of thermodynamics.

Here it is: Heat always flows from a hot substance to a cold one. The greater the difference in temperature, the faster the heat will be lost. It will also be lost faster if air passes over the surface rather than remains still (the old wind-chill factor). A thick coat does act as an insulator, helping to keep the dog's body temperature safe from cooling on frigid and even windy days. But on warm days, it also prevents contact with the outer air and wind, so a dog with a thick coat doesn't lose heat as rapidly as it would like to.

When the dog can no longer rely on losing enough body heat through its skin, it resorts to panting, which moves cooler air into the lungs, where it picks up heat and is then exhaled, and to the evaporative cooling process in play from saliva on the tongue. The problem is that panting takes a lot of energy, and like any exercise, also builds up heat. And there's but so much saliva that can be evaporated before your dog runs out. That's when heat prostration starts to set in.

That being said, Maggie will argue that a dog that is brushed out will lose most of the insulative undercoat, and the top coat acts more like the loose-fitting garments you see Bedouins wear. The top coat protects the skin that can easily be sunburned. The major problem with shaving is that a long-coated dog often takes his time growing back his top coat and may not have enough fur to protect him during the coming winter.

Shaving your dog's fur will help keep him cool in the summertime, and help prevent heat prostration. Keeping him brushed out will be effective as well, especially if it takes a long time for the fur to grow back. But don't cut the fur too short; the fur, like a thin shirt, does help protect against sunburn. Besides, you don't want to embarrass him by making him walk around totally naked in public. Just a summer outfit will be fine. 🐾

Do dogs sweat?

WHO WANTS TO CUDDLE WITH A SWEATY DOG? And what good will sweat do under all that fur? So dogs don't sweat, at least not like people do. They mostly regulate their temperature by panting. They inhale air of the ambient temperature into the lungs, where it is warmed to near-body temperature and exhaled. This means the cooler the air, the greater the temperature loss per breath. Panting is also effective because it cools the core of the body, rather than the outside skin, like sweating does. When the dog is hot, his tongue swells in size, so it accommodates more blood that can then be cooled by contact with the air. Saliva on the tongue cools by evaporation, so a hot dog also tends to salivate more. When you see a dog that is panting rapidly, with a swollen tongue and lots of spit, he's overheated and, if possible, you should get him to a cool place or into water.

Dogs sweat through the pads of their feet, so if you feel the pads of a hot dog, they may feel moist. It's often claimed that hairless breeds do actually sweat all over their body, and as a result tend to pant less, but breeders of hairless dogs we've spoken to say this isn't true.

Dogs that are exercising hard can raise their body temperature to extremely high levels, up to 108 degrees Fahrenheit (compared with a normal temperature of 101 to 102 degrees). But they avoid brain damage because they have a mechanism called a *rete mirabile*, which is a knot of small intermingled blood vessels at the base of the neck, which thermally isolates the head from the rest of the body where the muscles are generating all that heat. This allows the dog's brain to be shielded from the heat its own muscles make, but not from ambient heat.

Some dogs are more adversely affected by heat than others. Dogs with short snouts have less respiratory area over which to lose heat, and are especially prone to overheating. Large dogs with chunky builds are able to conserve heat more than small dogs with slender builds because, even though they don't sweat, they still lose some heat via dissipation through the skin. Smaller, leaner dogs have more skin surface compared with body mass and lose more heat than dogs with less surface area compared with mass.

But you don't have to pull out a calculator and formulate body mass versus surface area before deciding whether it's too hot to take your dog out. Just play it safe. In warm, especially humid, weather, don't exercise your dog. Give him access to a cool area and lots of water. This is one case where it pays to sweat the small stuff. 🐾

Do dogs get pimples?

HITTING THE TEENAGE YEARS can be really tough, especially if acne rears its ugly blackhead. Once again, it looks like our dogs have lucked out, but guess again. Dogs, too, can get acne and blackheads—and can get them at as early as three months of age. The acne usually appears on the chin and lower lip, but can also be on the groin area.

Acne occurs in some breeds more than in others, including boxers, bulldogs, and Great Danes. Hairless breeds, however, are those most afflicted with the social pain of acne and blackheads.

To treat those unsightly pimples, it's best to have your vet prescribe an acne wash and ointment. Of course, even with clear skin, there's still no guarantee he'll get a date. 🐾

Do dogs get goose bumps?

YOU'VE NO DOUBT HAD GOOSE BUMPS when you were cold, scared, or otherwise aroused. They're caused by tiny arrector pili muscles that contract and cause the hair follicles to rise up and stand erect in relation to your skin. What about your dog?

Dogs also have these arrector pili muscles, but they're pretty much restricted to the top of the neck, back, and tail. That's why when a dog raises his hackles, he doesn't get puffed up all over, but just along his top side. But what's under those hackles? Are they really goose bumps?

Now, don't try this at home (as we have), but if you scare your dog until his hackles stand up, and then reach under his fur and feel, you might expect there would be little goose bumps at the base of the hairs (you might also expect you'd get a dog bite). There aren't (and we didn't).

But maybe we just couldn't feel those bumps through all that fur. So we turned to breeders of hairless dogs and asked them, since they clearly should be able to see any goose bumps. They told us no, their hairless dogs don't get goose bumps in cold weather, even though they do get very cold. And yes, they appear to try to raise their hairless hackles, but when they do, the area just becomes wrinkled, not bumpy.

The verdict? No, dogs don't get goose bumps. 🐾

Do dogs get warts?

YOU SEE YOUR PUPPY PLAYING WITH A TOAD. Oh no! Well, you should be alarmed, because some toads can secrete a poisonous substance that can make small dogs sick; the giant marine toad can even kill a small dog. But even if your dog is prone to toad licking, the one thing you won't have to worry about is warts.

That's not to say dogs don't get warts. They do. But they don't get them from toads, and they also don't get them from people. Dog warts and people warts are caused by different viruses that aren't contagious between the two species. Dog warts, which are actually more correctly called *canine viral papillomas,* can be spread from dog to dog, however, and are most often seen on the lips of young dogs that still have immature immune systems. They'll usually go away on their own, but they can also be surgically removed. (It's hard to get a dog to leave a wart remover on his lips.) Meanwhile, don't worry. You can still kiss his warty lips without fear of catching warts. Or of turning into a toad. 🐾

Do dogs have belly buttons?

BELLY BUTTONS ARE SIMPLY THE PLACE where the umbilical cord was attached, and since dogs are born with umbilical cords, yes, they have belly buttons. But dog belly buttons tend to be small and unnoticeable, which is why they seldom elect to have them pierced.

Most dogs have innies, but some dogs have outies. Outies are referred to as *umbilical hernias*, and can be of two types. One type can be pushed back inside out so it looks like an innie, but it will push its way back out; the other type can't be pushed back in. The first type, which is called *reducible*, is actually dangerous for your dog, because it means the abdominal wall is still open, which in turn means it could one day constrict itself around the protruding tissues and strangulate them. Such a dog needs belly-button surgery to fix it. And here you always thought you'd be saving your money for your own plastic surgery! 🐾

Can a dog's eye really pop out of his head?

YOU'VE HEARD IT BEFORE: "You're going to put somebody's eye out!" But can an eye actually pop right out of its socket? It can, especially if you're a dog with a flat face.

Proptosis, as it's called, is when the eyeball is shoved forward so the lids pop closed behind it. The eye doesn't go bouncing around on the floor; it's still attached by several muscles as well as the big optic nerve leading to the brain. And the dog can still see out of it—for now.

The recipe for proptosis is a flat face, shallow eye socket, and big eye opening. Add to this a grab on the nape of the neck, or anything that pulls the skin back from the eyes, and a shake, and the result can be eye-popping (sorry). This most often happens when a big dog grabs a small dog, or when a person shakes or holds a small dog by the nape of the neck.

If this happens, you had better stop your screaming and start doing something helpful, because the longer the eye's hanging out there, the more likely it's going to end up blind. You can try to ease it back in place, but you probably can't. Keep the eye moist and get the dog to the emergency vet. 🐾

Can dogs suck out of a straw?

NO. Why would you want one to? 🐾

Why don't dogs get hair balls?

DOGS CAN GET HAIR BALLS, but not with the same frequency as cats. Cats get hair balls because they groom themselves by licking with their tongue, which has small barbs on it that catch the hair. Dogs can also lick themselves, but it's generally sporadic, and their tongue has no such barbs. So while they may end up swallowing some hair, especially if they have an itchy spot and chew the hair off, they don't usually swallow enough to cause problems. If your dog is hacking and coughing, a hair ball should be at the very bottom of your list of possible causes. He needs to be seen by a veterinarian to rule out a more serious problem. 🐾

Do dogs get tonsillitis?

LIKE PEOPLE, dogs have tonsils, which are small masses of tissue in the throat that help protect the body from invading microbes. Because they're part of the body's immune system, they can swell when the dog is ill due to entirely other reasons. Repeated vomiting, coughing, or excessive swallowing from some other causes can all bring on tonsillitis. But sometimes, especially in young dogs of small breeds, tonsillitis is the primary problem.

Signs of tonsillitis are retching, coughing, head shaking, repeated swallowing, and fever. The tonsils are red and inflamed. Antibiotics are the first course of treatment, but sometimes dogs must have a tonsillectomy. Break out the ice cream. 🐾

Do dogs get appendicitis?

NO, because dogs don't have an appendix. 🐾

Do dogs catch colds?

IT'S COLD AND FLU SEASON AGAIN and you're stuck in bed, sniffling and sneezing, when your annoyingly healthy dog comes to share some kisses. Should you go ahead and kiss him on the lips? Why doesn't he ever seem to share the misery of a cold?

Well, I've got good news—if you're a dog. The common cold basically comprises a hundred or so viruses that infect humans and other primates. The ones that cause colds in humans and other primates don't happen to infect dogs. So, your dog can't get a cold from you, nor can he give you one. Go ahead, give him a big kiss. Nobody else is going to kiss you, not with that runny nose. 🐾

Do dogs get the flu?

SO, IF DOGS DON'T GET COLDS, you're probably thinking that they don't get the flu. Several years ago, we would've been in agreement with you because there hadn't been any recent strains of dog flu to speak of.

Well, just when we thought we had it figured out, Greyhounds at a track in Florida came down with influenza. It appears that a type of horse flu mutated and infected dogs, with lethal results. Dog flu is a serious and highly contagious strain, with a mortality rate of 5 to 8 percent.

The good news is that dog flu is relatively rare, and healthy dogs can generally overcome it with some veterinary treatment. If your dog is coughing, he's more likely to have kennel cough than dog flu, but if his health starts to go downhill, this falls in the better-safe-than-sorry category. Call your vet. 🐾

Why do dogs get gas so often?

THE DOG DID IT. Really. And chances are, he probably did. Of course, part of the reason he gets the blame so often is that he doesn't even try not to pass gas in public. In fact, he seems to enjoy the entire experience, maybe sticking his nose down closer for a better whiff of his odiferous masterpiece.

The amount of gas a dog has may have to do with his breed or diet. That's because a fart is made up partly of gases from swallowed air, partly of components of ingested food, and partly of by-products of bacterial fermentation. Certain breeds, most notably the flat-faced ones, have earned a reputation for gassiness, in part because they tend to swallow air when gulping down their food. Dogs eat diets rich in protein, and proteins contain lots of sulfur, which is a major component of the stink in farts. In addition, some of the stink is made by bacterial fermentation in the gut. Certain carbohydrates that dogs cannot naturally digest increase the amount of gut fermentation, and thus, gas. If your dog farts a lot, you can try different diets, and you can try feeding him from a bowl that discourages gulping. Sometimes placing a large rock in the bottom of the bowl, so he has to eat around it, will do the trick. Just don't let him eat the rock!

By the way, why do dog farts tend to be silent (if deadly)? Some researchers (are there really flatulence researchers?) believe it has to do with the fact that a dog's anus is not at the bottom of his body, but at the rear. This means his anal sphincter doesn't have to be as tight as a human one, because it doesn't have to contend with the pressure caused by gravity that the sphincter at the bottom of our bodies has. A less tight sphincter means the anal opening doesn't vibrate as much when the gas escapes. It could also be that the dog's fart, while excelling in quality, isn't nearly the equal of the human fart in quantity. All of these are still theories, though, and the Nobel Prize surely awaits the intrepid scientist who can get to the bottom of this. 🐾

Does a dog's stomach rumble when he's hungry?

HERE'S SOMETHING ELSE YOU CAN blame on the dog. Because, just like you, her stomach rumbles. In fact, maybe more so. But actually, it doesn't growl when she's hungry, although she may very well be hungry at the same time. It growls when it's empty and the stomach walls still squeeze together in an attempt to mix and digest food. That makes the gases and digestive juices slosh around in the empty stomach, causing all sorts of gurgling and growling, or if you want to use the technical term, *borborygmi*. The cure is to get some food in that dog! 🐾

Can dogs be right-pawed or left-pawed?

ARE YOU HAVING DIFFICULTY TEACHING your dog basic penmanship? Maybe you're forcing him to use his wrong paw. Fortunately, a team of scientists has tackled the vital question of whether dogs are right- or left-pawed. They did this by sticking a strip of tape over the middle of a dog's snout, and then recording which paw the dog used to dislodge it. Interestingly, male dogs tended to be left-pawed and females tended to be right-pawed. Only a few were ambidextrous. Some studies have suggested that the male hormone testosterone is associated with left-handedness, and this study supports that idea. The study also found that dogs had differences in their immune systems according to whether they were left- or right-pawed. More importantly, the study has far-reaching implications for teaching your dog to write. Be sure to allow him to hold the pencil in whatever paw he feels most comfortable with. This way his penmanship will be its best, and he will not feel embarrassed. 🐾

Can dogs break their collarbone?

NO, because dogs don't have a collarbone. At least, not one that's worth noticing. Clavicles are important for primates because we use our arms to swing, but clavicles aren't important for animals, like dogs, that use their front legs for running. So the dog has only a rudimentary clavicle, less than an inch long, that seldom even appears on X-rays, and is too little even to break. 🐾

Why do dogs have wet noses?

DOGS HAVE WET NOSES for more reasons than just to jolt you awake on a chilly morning. Like most other *macrosmatic* animals (that is, animals with a very good sense of smell), dogs have a *rhinarium*—that's the technical term for the area of moist, furless skin that we usually refer to as the dog's nose. Researchers believe that the moist surface attracts and dissolves odor molecules, making them easier for your dog to smell.

Of course, there's another, older theory that goes back to Noah's Ark. It seems the two dogs on the ark were cruising around, poking their noses into everything as dogs do, when they discovered a leak in the hull. One dog went for help while the other stuck his nose in the hole to plug it. God conferred upon all dogs from then on wet noses as a badge of honor and permission to nudge us awake on a frosty morning. 🐾

Do dogs get boogers?

HAVE YOU EVER SEEN A DOG PICK ITS NOSE? No. That's because they don't have anything to pick. At least not usually. The dog's nose normally has a clear watery discharge, which probably keeps the nasal passages cleared sufficiently for boogers not to form. Boogers are actually partially dried mucus that forms around trapped dust particles. In the dog, the constant flow of watery mucus may flush out the thicker mucus and dust. Dogs seldom have snot, either. But dogs with allergies or nasal infections can have a thick mucus discharge (snot); if your dog has this, he needs to see a vet. And get some hankies. 🐾

Can you tickle a dog?

CAROLINE: I'VE TRIED. Repeatedly. But I've never gotten a reaction from a dog that I'd say is analogous to the human reaction of being tickled. Sure, the dog may try to get away. But laugh and squirm uncontrollably? No. That's not to say that animals can't be ticklish. Rats and some primates appear to be ticklish. But so far, nobody's demonstrated it in dogs. Go on, try. Better yet, just go buy a Tickle Me Fido.

Maggie: I've tickled dog toes with much success. All you have to do is tickle the hair on their toes and they jump and wriggle their paws away. But I don't recommend this in large part because it's a good way to get bit.

Caroline: I agree they can't stand to have their paw pads, or the hair on the bottoms of their feet, touched lightly. But they never seem to laugh when they're jerking their feet away. 🐾

Do dogs get hiccups?

YES! DOGS, ESPECIALLY PUPPIES, commonly get hiccups. Hiccups are sudden spasms of the diaphragm and can be caused by eating too fast and swallowing air, or eating very cold or fatty food. Sometimes the reason just isn't clear.

Trying all the common home remedies for people is pretty useless with dogs. Have you ever tried to make a puppy breathe into a paper sack or drink from the wrong side of a glass? And if you scared him, you'd just look like an ogre to your friends, scaring a poor hiccupping puppy. Anyway, it doesn't work, either. I've tried. 🐾

Do dogs' legs ever fall asleep?

YOU KNOW THE FEELING: You sit in a funny position, get up, and your leg is numb, so you hobble around until it starts tingling and the feeling finally returns. This usually happens because you put pressure on certain nerves, or blood vessels that lead to these nerves, temporarily putting them out of commission. If it happens to people, it must happen to dogs. But I have seldom, if ever, seen one of my dogs get up and start gimping around. Then again, if he did that, his lameness would probably be attributed to arthritis or some sort of temporary hitch in his get-along. So while dogs can't tell us their leg is asleep, it's a good bet it happens.

Maggie has seen her dogs have their legs asleep more than once. They really get silly trying to get up with it and wave it around like people do until they can walk properly on it. 🐾

Do dogs snore?

MOST PEOPLE WHO LIVE WITH BULLDOGS and their kin can answer this one: Yes! Flat-faced breeds are notorious for their snoring, usually because of a condition called an elongated soft palate, in which the palate extends too far into the throat and flaps around when the dog breathes. In severe cases, the dog's ability to breathe or sleep is compromised, and he needs surgery to shorten the palate and perhaps widen the nostrils. He'll sleep better. And so will you. 🐾

Does sugar make dogs hyperactive?

ASK JUST ABOUT ANY PARENT, and they'll tell you that sugar makes their kids wired. Ask most scientists, and they'll tell you there's little, if any, evidence that that's really the case. There's even less evidence that this happens in dogs. That doesn't mean you should ply your dog with sugar cubes. That's still unhealthy eating. But if you want to blame his bad behavior on something, look to his genes—or your training methods. 🐾

Can dogs have low blood sugar?

YOU MAY FEEL LIKE YOU'RE SUFFERING from low blood sugar if you've gone more than an hour without a cola, but chances are, you'll get over it. But if you're a dog, particularly a small puppy of a tiny breed, low blood sugar (more technically known as *hypoglycemia*) can be deadly. And it is more common than you might think.

Tiny puppies, as well as some adults of toy breeds, can't store enough readily available glycogen (which is the form in which the body stores glucose), and when the glycogen runs out, the body breaks down fat for energy. But because puppies have very little fat on their bodies, this energy store is also quickly depleted. When that happens, the brain, which depends on glucose to function, starts having problems. The puppy may start to get weak and sleepy, perhaps wobbling and stumbling about if forced to move. If he still gets no glucose, he can have seizures, lose consciousness, and die.

That's why it's so important that you not let your tiny puppy go more than four hours without eating. If that's not possible, such as in the middle of the night, make sure he's warm, confined, and quiet so that he doesn't use much energy.

Next, make sure you're feeding him foods that are fairly high in protein, fat, and complex carbohydrates. Complex carbs slow the breakdown of carbohydrates into sugars. This steady breakdown leads to more efficient use, rather than a roller-coaster ride of highs and lows. Avoid simple sugars, such as sweets and semimoist foods.

However, keep some on hand because they can be useful if your pup starts showing signs of hypoglycemia.

If you suspect your dog is becoming hypoglycemic, you need to get some simple sugars into him. Corn syrup is a good choice, but he probably won't swallow it. Rub it on his gums and the roof of his mouth. He may eat semimoist foods, so try that. Don't put anything in his mouth that could choke him! Keep him warm and call your veterinarian. If you've gotten enough sugar into him, he should start showing signs of improvement while you're still on the phone— within a couple of minutes. He may still need to go to the clinic for intravenous glucose. Once he's better and can eat, give him a small, high-protein meal, such as meat baby food.

For most dogs, hypoglycemia is just a puppyhood concern and will be outgrown by the age of seven months or so. 🐾

Will a convulsing dog swallow his tongue?

NO. IT'S AN OLD WIVES' TALE about both people and dogs that some-one having a convulsion can swallow his tongue.

Dogs seem to suffer from a high rate of seizures, whether from epilepsy, toxicity, low blood sugar, brain tumors, or unknown causes. The best you can do is move them away from stairways or furniture that can be knocked over, and get any other dogs out of the room. The sight of a convulsing dog can sometimes cause even its best doggy friend to attack. Write down a description of how the dog acted before and during the seizure, which can help your veterinarian diagnose the cause. Most seizures stop within a couple of minutes, but one that keeps going beyond that can be deadly, causing fatal overheating or irreversible brain damage unless you get him to the veterinarian so the seizure can be stopped. 🐾

Do dogs ever bite their own tongue?

"IF YOU DIDN'T EAT WITH YOUR MOUTH OPEN, you wouldn't bite your own tongue." That's what I was always told. But then look at how dogs eat. With jaws flapping and food dribbling, they give "see food" a whole new meaning.

Then again, some of them don't chew food enough to really make an issue of it; they seem more likely to swallow their own tongues than bite them.

But dogs do occasionally bite their own tongues. Fortunately, they don't seem to chomp down too hard, or they might end up tongue-less. They seem to bite them less often than people bite their own tongues, perhaps because with constantly hanging it out of their mouths, they naturally have a mechanism that automatically pulls it from the path of their own teeth. Or maybe they are just too cool to let on that they bit it. 🐾

Can a dog live without a tongue?

A DOG WITHOUT A TONGUE? It might seem that a dog without a licker would miss out on some of the best parts of being a dog. And that may be true. But tongueless dogs do manage to get along. True, they can't stop themselves from drooling, they can't lick themselves, or you, and they can't lap water. But they can learn to drink by immersing their snout in a fluid, and to eat by throwing the food to the back of their throat.

Dogs can lose their tongues from cancer, or from accidents such as chewing an electric cord or licking metal on a freezing day—and then freaking out and ripping off their own tongue. Yes, it's happened more than once. This is why plastic buckets are better than metal ones in cold weather. 🐾

Are some dogs' bites more dangerous than others'?

WELL, WHICH WOULD YOU RATHER BE BITTEN BY, a Pekingese or a Rottweiler? Of course, some dogs' bites are more dangerous. Just how much more so is a matter of dispute. Claims abound as to the biting strength of pit bulls, but the truth is, no real study has ever compared dog bite strength. Of course, if you'd like to volunteer your arm, perhaps it could be arranged. Meanwhile, you'd have to get them to clamp down on a pressure plate, which could be done, although some would no doubt do it more enthusiastically than others.

Lacking actual data (and since when did that ever stop us?), we can make an educated guess about bite strength. Bigger teeth mean bigger holes, in general. Wider heads also mean stronger bites. The muscles that control jaw closure run along the sides of the face, through the *zygomatic arch* (that's the bone you can feel below and to the outside of each eye) and up to a ridge of bone on top of the skull. You can feel or sometimes see this muscle moving as your dog chews. The wider the head, the more room for these muscles, and the stronger the jaws. Of course, just because a dog can bite hard doesn't mean he will. But that's another story.

Are dogs with blue eyes blind, deaf, or crazy?

IN A WORD, NO. Well, maybe crazy, but no more so than most dogs. And actually, there's a little more to the story. Blue eyes result from an absence of pigment in the iris, and it's not that uncommon to find a dog with two blue eyes, one blue eye, or one or two partially blue eyes. Blue eyes are common with some of the coat colors associated with deafness in dogs, but just because a dog has blue eyes doesn't mean he's deaf. However, in some breeds, such as Dalmatians, English

Setters, and English Cocker Spaniels, dogs with blue eyes are statisti-
cally more likely to be deaf. As for blindness, so far nobody has
demonstrated any difference at all between the vision of blue-eyed
dogs and others. But they do look kind of crazy. 🐾

Why are dogs' eyes reflective, and do the colors mean anything?

IF YOU SHINE A LIGHT INTO YOUR DOG'S EYE, part of that light is actually absorbed by the visual photoreceptors (rods and cones), which
send a nerve impulse in response and allow your dog to see. But part
of the light manages to sneak past the photoreceptors, only to hit a
reflective surface behind the retina, the *tapetum lucidum*. The tapetum sends the light back through the photoreceptors for a second
chance at absorption, but once again, some of the light sneaks past
and now comes right back out the pupil. No, it's not like your dog has
beams of light shining from his eyeballs, so don't get any ideas about
throwing away your flashlights and just aiming Chihuahuas down a
dark path.

The only way you can see this light is to be lined up so as to be
looking straight down into the dog's pupils. This is what happens
when you take a flash picture with your camera, and it's why your
dog's eyes may glow red, green, yellow, or blue. Some people think the
color indicates the dog's emotional state, sort of like a built-in mood
ring. But it doesn't. The tapetum of individual dogs tends to be of different colors, and that's why some dogs have green eye shine in photos and others have yellow. And just because your dog may have a red
eye shine doesn't mean he's seeing red; he may be a dog without a
tapetum, in which case the red comes from blood vessels at the rear
of the eyeball. 🐾

Can all dogs swim?

ASK MOST PEOPLE AND they would say of course! But that can be a potentially fatal assumption. Some dogs simply have the buoyancy of cinderblocks. Bulldogs, French Bulldogs, Pugs, Pekingese, and other breeds with similar heavy-fronted body builds simply sink like rocks. No amount of swimming lessons will help them float. If you have one of these breeds, it's essential that you fence off your swimming pool so they can't fall in.

Other dogs need a little help swimming, but they can stay afloat. New swimmers tend to try to walk on water with their front feet, which makes their rear end sink. You can help them learn the correct dog paddle technique by lifting their rear end up to the surface level and placing a hand at water level so the front feet can't break the surface. Once they catch on, they'll be swimming right along like pros. Even so, they can't swim forever, and again, if you have a swimming pool, either fence it off or make sure you teach your dog to swim to the steps to get out.

And if your dog goes boating, or swimming anywhere that might prove too much for him, have him wear a doggy life vest. It could save his life, and he'll look quite fashionable in it. 🐾

Can dogs swim underwater?

YOU'VE PROBABLY KNOWN DOGS that can poke their snout or head underwater and come up with a rock or ball, but what about actually swimming underwater? Yep, many dogs can dive clear to the bottom of a swimming pool and retrieve objects—automatic pool sweepers are a favorite target!

Dogs can even walk along the shore and find items underwater. They do this by smelling the item when they're still above water; then they hold their breath, open their eyes, and dive! 🐾

Is the fastest dog faster than the fastest horse?

WANT TO START A FIGHT? Ask this question in the middle of a group of horse and dog racing fans. So at a race track in the United Kingdom, officials decided to put it to the test. They raced a top Greyhound against a top thoroughbred over a 400-meter grass course. The Greyhound won by seven (horse) lengths. To be fair, it was the dog's jackrabbit start that was the key, and the horse was steadily gaining. Had the course been longer, the horse would have overtaken the Greyhound, which is known for its sprinting, not its endurance.

Estimates place the horse world's best sprinter, the quarter horse, at forty-seven miles per hour, and the Greyhound at a mere forty-one miles per hour. The Greyhound's running style is more like that of a cheetah's, employing what's known as the double-suspension gallop. Unlike horses, which have only one period during their galloping stride in which all four legs are off the ground at once (the period when they are all contracted beneath the body), Greyhounds and many other fast dogs have two periods of suspension during their fastest gallop: the contracted phase, like the horse, plus the extended phase, like the picture of the Greyhound on the side of the bus. This bounding gallop helps them go faster, but it also eats up energy and so cannot be sustained for long. 🐾

What's the purpose of that footpad way up at the top of the dog's wrist?

IF YOU FEEL BEHIND YOUR DOG'S FRONT LEG, where his foreleg meets his wrist, you'll find a footpad just like the ones on the bottom of your dog's feet. This pad, called the *stopper pad* (technically, the carpal pad) may seem to be in a strange place, way up there on the leg, until you see stop-action films of a dog running at high speed. The wrist

79

joint actually bends so that the entire foot and wrist, clear up to the stopper pad, are on the ground. So the stopper pad functions just as any other footpad does, but only comes into play at high speed. 🐾

Can dogs have extra toes, like some cats do?

YOU'VE SEEN CATS WITH SIX TOES (called *polydactyl* cats), so you may be wondering if dogs can have six or more toes. The answer is, yes! In fact, some breed standards, such as the Great Pyrenees and the Norwegian Lundehund (Puffin Dog) actually *require* the dog have extra toes.

It's normal for dogs to have four toes on the hind feet and five on the front feet. Some dogs that are used for show or hunting will have the fifth toe on the front foot, commonly called the dewclaw, taken off for a cleaner look or to avoid getting it caught on things. This toe is homologous to our thumb, but unlike our thumb, in many dogs it is loosely attached and doesn't give the dog much gripping power.

Some breeds, such as Great Pyrenees, naturally have one or two dewclaws on their rear feet as well. And at least one breed, the Norwegian Lundehund, has at least six toes on each foot. These dogs climbed the craggy rocks in search of puffin birds, using their extra toes to help keep a good grip. If only Ernest Hemingway had known about them. 🐾

Do some dogs have webbed feet?

IF IT LOOKS LIKE A DUCK, and quacks like a duck—it might just be a Newfoundland or Labrador Retriever. Oddly enough, some water breeds, such as the Newfoundland and some Labrador Retrievers, have more webbing in their feet, thus making it easier for them to dog paddle than other dogs.

So, yes, Virginia, some dogs do have webbed feet. 🐾

How do three-legged dogs get around?

THEY HOP. Depending on the dog's body structure, getting around on three legs may or may not be a challenge. The heavier the dog, and wider the body, the harder it is, especially if it's a front leg that's missing. A dog's weight is centered toward the front of its body, so the front legs do most of the weight-bearing. A dog that's missing a hind leg can simply aim the remaining one toward the centerline and balance on it quite easily. Some three-legged dogs can race, swim, catch Frisbees, and do almost anything a four-legged dog can do. 🐾

Can a dog with only two legs get around?

DOGS ARE OCCASIONALLY BORN WITH ONLY HIND LEGS. These dogs are often raised and can learn to walk on their hind legs, sort of like people. Such dogs have often appeared throughout the years in circuses and other entertainment venues. Other dogs have lost legs through accidents. An Italian Greyhound named Dominic lost both legs on one side, yet could run and leap like a four-legged dog. 🐾

Do all big dogs have bad hips?

IT'S TRUE THAT LARGE DOGS may have hip dysplasia. But not all large dogs have bad hips. Certain breeds tend to be almost immune from hip dysplasia, most notably those in the sight hound family. Greyhounds, although large, almost never have hip dysplasia, and even their larger cousins like Borzoi and Scottish Deerhounds rarely are affected. Some researchers believe the high muscle mass of these breeds may be related to the low hip dysplasia incidence, but others believe it has to do with certain non–hip-dysplasia genes that these breeds were lucky enough to inherit. Certainly, had these dogs been afflicted with bad hips in the days when they were being created, they would not have lasted long on the coursing field, and would never have made it into the gene pool.

The Orthopedic Foundation for Animals is the largest registry of hip data in the world. The breeds with the highest percentage of hip dysplasia in their database are, first, the Bulldog, followed by the Pug, Dogue de Bordeaux, Otterhound, Neapolitan Mastiff, Saint Bernard, Clumber Spaniel, Black Russian Terrier, Sussex Spaniel, and Cane Corso. While not all of these would be considered large dogs, they are all certainly heavy-bodied dogs. But before you rush out and buy a little dog just to avoid hip problems, remember, little dogs have their own problems. They're far more likely to have bad knees and a hip condition that is just as bad as hip dysplasia. Which just goes to show, if it's not one thing it's another. 🐾

Why are some breeds' tails docked?

DOCKING THE TAIL DATES BACK at least to the ancient Romans, who docked tails to remove tendons, which were thought to be worms causing rabies. Docking has since been performed on fighting dogs so that their tails could not be grabbed, on working dogs to identify them as nontaxable working animals, on long-haired dogs to prevent fecal matter from becoming caught in the coat, on terriers to provide a sturdy handle for pulling them out of a burrow, and on bird dogs to prevent tail injuries in the field.

Today there are fewer arguments for docking. Docking is usually done for cosmetic and breed-standard purposes, although hunting and hygiene also play a factor. Breeders of traditionally docked breeds prefer the look, and worry that undocked tails may vary in appearance because tails have never been subjected to selection. Hygiene can still be a problem, especially in inadequately groomed pets. Yuck! Tail trauma, often caused by vigorous tail wagging while hunting in brambles, is still a problem for gundogs. Tails do not heal well, and injuries sometimes result in amputation, a painful procedure for an adult dog. Perhaps the best reason to dock a tail, though, is so that mean kids can't pull it!

Veterinary surveys show tail injuries are not widespread among all breeds (one survey showed that most cases involved complications following docking). However, a Swedish survey of gundog breeders following the prohibition of docking there found that 51 percent of the dogs had sustained tail injuries in the three years following the ban, with seven dogs requiring amputation. 🐾

Does docking a dog's tail throw off his balance?

WHAT DOES A TAIL DO? You often hear it is used as a rudder, or as an aid to balance, and on the surface, these notions make sense. But if you try to track down these tales of the tail, you find there is not one shred of actual evidence to support these ideas. Dogs with docked tails seem to balance just as well as dogs with long tails. It's true that dogs do seem to use their tails as a counterbalance when turning or braking at high speed, but even Greyhounds with amputated tails seem to corner and brake just as well as their natural-tailed cohorts. And short-tailed herding breeds such as Australian Shepherds and Pembroke Welsh Corgis seem to do just fine dancing out of the way of cattle's kicking hooves. Perhaps if we tested a group of tailed versus tailless dogs on a balance beam, we'd see a difference, but somehow I don't see the government handing out grants to investigate this question any time soon. 🐾

Does it hurt puppies when their tails are docked?

DOCKING IS PERFORMED DURING the first days of life because, at that stage, it can be done without anesthesia, whereas later in life it requires general anesthesia and a longer recovery. But does that mean it doesn't hurt for puppies? Breeders and veterinarians differ in their opinion of how painful the process is. In a survey, 25 percent of breeders and 0 percent of veterinarians believed newborn puppies could not feel pain; 76 percent of veterinarians (but only 18 percent of breeders) believed docking caused significant pain.

Those who believe newborns feel less pain base that assertion on several observations. First, the fatty insulation (myelin) that covers nerve fibers is not fully developed until several days after birth. However, nerve fibers carrying pain information tend to have little or no myelin throughout life, so this may not be a good index of nerve function. In fact, some research even suggests that puppies may feel pain more intensely than adults because the inhibitory pathway that serves to cancel out some of the pain messages develops only after the regular pain pathways develop and may not yet be present in neonates. Also, the density of pain receptors may actually be greater in the skin of newborns than in adults.

Second, breeders base their impressions of puppy pain perception on puppy behavior. Most pups undergoing docking will struggle and cry at the moment of docking and during suturing and continue to cry for an average of two minutes afterward. When placed back with the dam, they suckle and fall back to sleep, in contrast to sick pups that characteristically crawl about crying and will not suckle. But these observations may not be as consoling as we would like to think. A newborn cannot sustain vigorous vocalization over a long period without tiring. Suckling may in fact be a sign of acute pain, because it encourages the release of pain-fighting endorphins.

While most veterinarians cut the pup's tail off with surgical scissors, most breeders band the tail, cutting off the blood supply by placing a tight ligature around the tail. Most breeders consider banding to be relatively painless. No pain comparisons exist in dogs, but comparisons of cutting and banding of lamb tails suggest just the opposite: that banding produces greater total amounts of behavioral and physiological indices of pain. Evidence from lambs further suggests that giving an injection of something like novocaine right before banding lowers pain indications, yet such local anesthetics are seldom used when docking puppy tails.

Do-it-yourself tail docking, especially by novices, can be disastrous. Docking must be done at the junction between bones, but uneducated breeders have cut bones in half. In these unfortunate animals, infections have developed that have claimed the rest of the tail, or even the puppy. Docking must be done in accordance with the breed standard; you can't put part of the tail back on if you've taken off too much, nor can you keep whittling it down until you have it short enough. It's the job of a veterinarian experienced with docking a particular breed. Whether by cutting or banding, amputation is surgery, not a do-it-yourself kitchen job.

So while the question of how much pain a puppy feels during docking is up for grabs, it's certain they do feel some degree of pain. Then again, newborn boys are circumcised with some of the same painful questions surrounding them. Ouch! 🐾

Why don't breeders just breed tailless dogs if that's what they want?

WITH THE VAST VARIATION in dog bodies, wouldn't it be simpler just to breed tailless or short-tailed dogs rather than cut them to size? In fact, many breeds often have bobtailed dogs born to them already. Why not just breed from them?

This seems like a good idea, but it doesn't always work. For one thing, if you used only the natural bobs, as they're called, you'd have such a small gene pool in some breeds that you'd be inviting disaster and the breed's health would plummet. But the main reason is that, when you breed natural bobs to natural bobs, you get a variation in tail length, and occasionally some of the shorter ones have a shortened spine or even spina bifida. This does not seem to happen in all breeds, however, leading to the proposal that different genes may be responsible for short tails in different breeds.

One researcher has actually introduced the gene for natural bobtails into his line of Boxers. After five generations of crossing back to Boxers, the dogs look like typical purebred Boxers, often with natural bobtails. It's still too early in the experiment to ensure that no health problems will emerge, but it does offer a tantalizing possibility to people who may want short tails without docking. 🐾

Is one dog year equal to seven people years?

YOU'VE HEARD THE OLD ADAGE, one dog year equals seven people years. When considering a dog's age, you figure that a three-year-old dog is equal to a twenty-one-year-old, and a ten-year-old dog is equal to a seventy-year-old person. How reliable is that?

Not very. For one thing, it's tough to correlate dog ages into a formula. One reason is simply that different dog breeds age differently. For example, a Great Dane that lives past eight years of age is a very old dog indeed. He may start getting gray and arthritic at age five. On the other hand, a small dog breed, let's say a Chihuahua, can live to fifteen years or more, and not show signs of aging until well after ten.

Then, let's look at the seven-to-one correlation. According to this formula, at one year of age, the dog is equivalent to a seven-year-old child. But dogs become sexually mature somewhere between the age of six months and one year, thus making that concept invalid (not too many sexually mature seven-year-old children out there). At two years of age, a dog is supposed to be just like a fourteen-year-old in maturity. And yet, most reputable breeders agree that two years old is when a dog more or less finishes growing and maturing.

So, something is obviously wrong with the seven to one concept. Some veterinarians have tried to make the age a bit more realistic by saying a one-year-old dog is equal to a fifteen-year-old adolescent. A two-year-old dog is equal to a person who is about twenty-one. After that, you add four years for every one.

While this general rule sounds good at first thought, it doesn't work well in breeds that age fast. A Great Dane that lives to the ripe old age of ten is considered to be only fifty-three—not even old enough to get a senior discount. A dog that lives to his fifteenth year is only seventy-three by this model.

So, what do you do? Basically, you accept that dogs older than two years are adults, then look at the size and breed of the dog. Not quite the formula you were looking for, but a shade more accurate.

Will dog spit kill you faster than human spit?

"DOG SPIT! YUCK!" That was Lucy's reaction whenever Snoopy managed to get in a slurp. Then, Linus would try to tell her that dog spit was cleaner than human spit. Um, has he seen what dogs put into their mouths? So who's right? Is dog spit more dangerous or less dangerous than human spit?

This one is a little bit controversial. Back in the olden times, people would see dogs lick their wounds, and the wounds would often remain clean and heal up—at least better than the wounds people got. But any veterinarian will tell you that if your dog is wounded, you should keep him from licking his wounds. Why? Because there are plenty of germs that will cause infection to the wound if the dog licks it instead of it being kept properly bandaged. Compared with the antibiotic ointments available, even the most medicinal dog spit is no match. Besides, constant licking can expand a wound. That's why vets go so far as to give owners the dread Elizabethan collars to put on their pets while they're healing to prevent the dog from licking and chewing out stitches.

The reality is that dogs have plenty of germs in their mouths that can cause infection. In fact, when a dog bites, there are enzymes in the saliva that prevent proper healing. Anyone who has been bitten by a dog can tell you that the first thing doctors worry about is infection.

But which is worse, a bite from a dog or a bite from a person? People bites can carry nasty diseases caught from another person, and dog bites can carry nasty bacteria. The popular *Mythbusters* television show had a quick demonstration of who had more germs, a *Mythbuster* regular or a dog. Alarmingly, the person's saliva grew more germs in the petri dish than the dog's. Then again, who knows where those TV celebrities' mouths have been!

So what about dog kisses? I don't know about you, but I'd rather kiss a random dog off the street than a random bum. But it is true that you can get sick from microbes such as salmonella and campylobacter from a dog's mouth. Maybe you should just have him gargle first. 🐾

Are some dogs sneeze-free—for allergic people?

YOU'VE HEARD THE CLAIMS of some dogs being hypoallergenic, that is, able to be tolerated well by allergy sufferers. Maybe you've been looking for such a dog yourself. Are they out there, and can people with allergies tolerate certain dogs?

Lots of dogs have been purported to be hypoallergenic. These include Poodles, Cockapoos, Labradoodles, Soft Coated Wheaten

Terriers, Chow Chows, Chinese Crested, and others. There are several theories as to why these dogs are supposed to be hypoallergenic. One theory is that the single-coated breeds (that is, the dogs with virtually no undercoat) don't shed and therefore don't aggravate allergies—although Chow Chows have plenty of undercoat, so there goes that theory!

The reality is much more complex. Allergies aren't caused by hair tickling your nose, but by dander—microscopic particles of skin and hair. And dogs with the so-called single coat cannot only shed just as much but have just as much dander as double-coated dogs. But wait! The story doesn't stop there. Many allergy sufferers aren't allergic to the dog's dander or hair, but to the dog's saliva. So, even if you minimize the shedding, it's not the hair, it's the spit. And even some other people are allergic to components of dog urine, so if the dog pees in the house, they have even more to cry about.

Allergies are specific to individuals; what makes one person sneeze doesn't necessarily affect another. So if your friend with allergies suggests you get the same breed as she has because it's the one dog she's not allergic to, better check it out for yourself before you commit to a so-called hypoallergenic breed. And if you end up with a dog that makes you sneeze, go to the allergist. 🐾

Are some breeds really single-coated?

YOU'LL OFTEN HEAR PEOPLE talk about dogs with single or double coats. A double coat essentially refers to a dog that has both long, fairly coarse outer hairs, or guard hairs, with short, soft hair lying beneath it, the undercoat. But it may not be quite that simple.

Dog hair grows in bundles of three to six hairs that all come out of the same follicle in the skin. Each bundle usually consists of a single guard hair and a group of underhairs. Breeds differ as regards the density of bundles in the skin and over how many hairs are in each bundle. For example, smooth Dachshunds and Toy Poodles have 400 to 600 bundles per square centimeter, while German Shepherds and Airedales have only 100 to 300.

The bundles are made up of six different hair types, including a long straight hair, shorter bristle hair, and on down to a fine wavy hair. These hair types, along with the angle at which the hair is implanted into the skin, can account for the variation in coat in almost all breeds. One exception is that wire-haired breeds have a seventh hair type not seen in other coat types. Short-haired breeds have very little undercoat hairs. Dogs with long, silky hair have a preponderance of the long, straight-type hairs, with very few bristle hairs. Poodles actually have a long, wavy hair type that suggests their coat is made up of all undercoat, rather than the more familiar outercoat. Their coat tends to have a longer growth cycle, but each hair grows in spurts.

So while it appears that many breeds have a greater proportion of outer hairs or undercoat, it's likely that most breeds have at least some of each. Still, it's close enough to label some as single-coated. 🐾

Why do some dogs shed and others don't?

ARE YOU ONE OF THOSE picky people who doesn't like dog hair as a food condiment? Maybe you're thinking that a nonshedding dog might be the ticket for you. But is there any such thing?

Well, I have good news and bad news. The bad news is that there is pretty much no such thing as a completely nonshedding dog. Dogs that are purported to be nonshedding (Poodles, Soft Coated Wheaten Terriers, and the like) do lose hair. The good news is that they don't have the seasonal shedding cycle (or year-round shedding cycle, in many cases) that other dogs do, and lose hair as a natural course. The reason is that such dogs' coats are made up of hairs that grow for long periods of time before falling out, more like how human hair grows. And once it falls out, it often gets trapped in neighboring hairs, so it stays on the dog (and mats) rather than falling to your floor.

Shedding is controlled by several factors, including hormones, seasonal variation, and genetics. Following the whelping of puppies or an estrus period, female dogs undergo an intense shedding period. And dogs naturally shed twice a year, in the spring and fall. Shedding is greatly controlled by light periods, which is why indoor dogs also shed slightly all year long.

If you want a dog that won't shed at all, you can try one of the hairless breeds, but even these dogs have a small amount of hair, which could fall out. But if you're that persnickety, might I suggest a stuffed animal? 🐾

How do sled dogs sleep in the snow without freezing?

A WHILE BACK, Maggie was inundated with questions from folks asking her how on earth sled dogs can sleep in the snow and not freeze. Seems there was a movie that depicted this, and people asked the only musher they knew personally, namely Maggie.

Because Maggie has owned northern breeds most of her adult life, she feels pretty confident about the answer. Sled dogs are built to survive the cold because their fur is naturally insulative. So much so that you can watch a sled dog out in the snow get covered with the snow and not have it melt. That means the fur traps in all the dog's body heat, even in the coldest weather.

Northern breeds comprise what are called *double-coated dogs*. They have harsh guard hairs or an outercoat that repels moisture as well as a soft downy layer that traps the warm air and keeps it next to the dog's skin. Think of it as if you were wearing a thick down coat—only the dog wears it all the time.

When a sled dog sleeps in the snow, he will curl himself up in a ball, pressing the less thickly furred areas, such as the legs and head, closer to his belly and underside to conserve warmth. He'll even put his tail over his nose to keep that warm. As snow piles up around him, it forms even more insulation to keep his heat in, just like an igloo. Because his fur is so insulative, the snow doesn't melt on him and he doesn't get wet. Instead, he stays toasty warm.

How do dogs run on snow without their feet freezing?

WHILE WE'RE ON THE SUBJECT OF SLED DOGS, you may wonder how sled dogs run on snow without their feet freezing.

Most dogs, when they're out in the snow, get snowballs between their toes, and many dogs find the whole snow thing to be a bit on the chilly side. So, what makes sled dogs (and some other breeds) capable of running on the snow?

First, dogs have a higher body temperature than we do, that being 101.5 degrees Fahrenheit. Their paws are warmer. Second, many northern breeds have harsh coats that enable their fur to be especially snow- and ice-resistant. The oils in their hair naturally shed snow. As you know, oil and water don't mix, and neither does snow and husky hair because of the difference in consistency.

However, some huskies have the softer, finer hair with less oil—and those *do* attract snowballs. So, how do mushers handle that one? First, they clip the hair around the foot so that there's less to collect snow. Then, if the dogs are traveling distances, they put booties on the dog—that is, little dog shoes that protect the feet. If the dogs are racing in shorter races, sometimes mushers use cooking spray (such as Pam) on the dog's feet. The cooking spray adds enough oil to keep the snow out of the fur. 🐾

How can dogs run a thousand miles or more in sledding competitions?

YOU'VE PROBABLY HEARD OF LONG-DISTANCE RACES such as the Iditarod or the Yukon Quest. These races go for a thousand miles or more. But you may wonder how these sled dogs can actually run that far when your dog can't make a trip around the block.

Four things enable a long-distance husky to go the distance. The first is breeding. These dogs are specially bred and have the proper build to run such distances. In other words, they're genetically predisposed to do just that. Their bodies are large enough to give them a good stride with good strength, but not so large that they need to carry around a lot of bulk, or burn even more calories, or perhaps most important, overheat. Their bodies are well muscled, but not overly bulked up. Their tissues are highly vascularized, the better to get blood to their cells. Even their blood is packed with a higher proportion of hemoglobin than most other breeds, so much so that a human athlete would be accused of blood-packing if they were discovered harboring such high amounts. But hemoglobin carries energy to cells, so dogs that run a long way need a lot of hemoglobin. The only other dogs to have such high levels are dogs in the Greyhound family, the sight hounds.

The second is training. Every year, these dogs run one thousand training miles or more, even before they get to the big race. They start out with itty-bitty runs of a mile or two and gradually work up to as much as a hundred miles at a time. This training period usually starts in August, which gives the dogs enough time until February or March to run the big races. Some mushers train year-round, using various techniques, such as running the dogs loose behind an all-terrain vehicle. Some mushers have built wheels that look like giant hamster wheels or merry-go-rounds that the dogs can run on if they like during the off-season.

The third is nutrition. These dogs are fed an extremely high-protein, high-fat diet that may include meat, fats, and extra vitamins. These diets—richer than anything you would feed your dog at home—help boost the energy of sled dogs.

The fourth is the musher's strategy. The musher has to plan rest stops so that the dogs get enough rest and calories to keep going and finish the race. No dog can run a thousand miles without some sort of respite, so it's important to the musher to be sure that the dogs get adequate rest for peak performance. 🐾

Can dogs be blood donors?

YOU MAY NOT HAVE SEEN the doggy bloodmobile parked outside the veterinary hospital, but that's not because doggy blood donors aren't needed. Most veterinary clinics keep their own blood donors in-house, either a clinic dog that lives there, the veterinarian's dog that comes to work every day, or a network of client dogs that have been volunteered to be "on call."

Blood donors have to be fairly large (no sense in sucking a Chihuahua dry to try to save a Saint Bernard!), calm enough to take blood from (it takes about fifteen to twenty-five minutes, using the jugular vein), free of blood parasites (they are routinely checked), and have red-cell–rich blood. The breed of choice is the Greyhound, because they meet all these criteria, and because there are usually Greyhounds in need of adoption from race tracks. Greyhounds have blood that is densely packed with red blood cells in comparison with other dogs. For example, a common measure of red blood cells, the hematocrit, averages around 35 percent in most dogs, but runs around 45 to 60 percent in greys. That's more bang for the buck, and helps anemic dogs get well faster. Many vets will keep an adopted greyhound as a donor for several months, then find it a home, replacing it with another dog from the track, so each dog eventually gets his chance at a home life.

Compatible blood can last three to four weeks in the recipient's body. An artificial blood, made from cow hemoglobin, is also available and has the advantage of being easily stored and readily available. However, it lasts in the recipient's body only about two days. 🐾

Do dogs have different blood types?

DOGS DO HAVE DIFFERENT BLOOD TYPES, but don't think you have to run out and get a medic alert bracelet so you'll be prepared in case of an accident. First, dogs have thirteen different blood types, and one dog can have more than one type.

Fortunately, dogs rarely have antibodies against other blood types, so it's usually safe to give a dog a blood transfusion without knowing its blood type first. However, dogs that have received a previous transfusion no longer have this luxury, because that transfusion may have activated antibodies that can now react fatally with a subsequent transfusion. Their blood must be cross-matched with a donor. In fact, females that have previously whelped a litter are also at higher risk and should always be cross-matched before receiving blood. 🐾

5

A Dog's
Senses

Can dogs smell fear?

YOU'RE WALKING DOWN A DARK ALLEY. A stray dog skulks out in front of you. You remember what your mother said: *Dogs can smell fear.* He sniffs the air. Are you dead meat?

Maybe, maybe not. Strictly speaking, fear is an emotion and can't be smelled. But as an emotion, fear can produce a wave of physiological reactions that could cause a change in the scent your body emits. When you're afraid, your autonomic nervous system prepares you for fight or flight by, among other things, dumping glucose into your bloodstream, increasing your breathing rate, and increasing your sweat gland activity. Any of these could conceivably cause changes in odor that could be perceived by a dog, but sweat is the most likely culprit. Sweat secretions carry cells that are broken down by bacteria, an action that produces what even we humans perceive as body odor. So when you're fearful, you sweat more, and when you sweat more, you stink more. And your dog knows.

So it's likely that when you're emotionally aroused, dogs can smell changes in how strong you smell, but it's hard to say if they can sense changes that occur from being scared versus those from being excited or happy. Nonetheless, many dog handlers in law enforcement believe dogs can smell fear, and one company even markets a human "fear and trauma" training scent for dogs.

So be afraid. Be very afraid. Better yet, don't. 🐾

Can dogs smell the difference between identical twins?

YOU'RE SITTING AT HOME ONE EVENING watching television. You hear baying outside and then a bullhorn: "This is the police. We've got you surrounded!" Once you've been cuffed, they explain that tracking dogs have followed your scent from a nearby crime scene. Sure enough, one of the dogs sniffs you and makes a positive ID. "But," you protest, "I didn't do it! It was my evil twin!" Will the jury buy it?

Maybe. At least three studies have asked just this question. In one study, dogs could tell identical twins apart but tended to make mistakes. In another, dogs could stay on the trail of one identical twin versus another, but would retrieve articles scented by either one interchangeably. Finally, a third study showed dogs could tell the difference between identical twins only if the twins lived in different places or ate different diets. So if you lived with your evil twin, ate the same foods, used the same laundry detergents, and bathed in the same soaps, you'd have a good case for mistaken identity. But if your evil twin lived somewhere else and the dogs still insisted you did it—I'm sure you'll make new friends in prison. Besides, if your identical twin is evil, wouldn't you be, too?

When a dog tracks somebody and starts in the middle, how does he know which way to go?

WE ALL KNOW DOGS CAN TRACK AN ODOR TRAIL from start to finish. But what if the dog doesn't know which way is the start and which is the finish? What if you're searching for a lost hiker and your tracking dog suddenly comes across his trail? He follows it to the left for a while. Then he follows it to the right. The dog's found the trail, but which way did he go? And if the dog sets out in one direction, can you really believe him?

Let's think about what clues the dog has to go on. He's tracking by scenting cells that have come from the hiker's body and clothes, and by scenting the disturbance of the ground wherever the hiker stepped. It makes sense that these might be more intense the fresher they were, so they'd get gradually stronger if the dog went in the same direction as the hiker. But such differences would have to be astronomically small!

Or perhaps the dog would have to smell a "footprint image," much as a human tracker would determine direction by looking at the direction the prints were facing.

Early studies concluded that dogs couldn't determine the direction of a track, but more recent studies showed that if you used dogs trained to seek out the right direction, they could indeed identify which way the track was headed. You couldn't even fool these dogs by giving them visual cues indicating the track went the other way. That still left open the question of how. If you use some inanimate object solely to disturb the layout of the ground, the dogs can't figure out which way the track goes, so they're not relying on differences in scent from ground disturbance.

If you have a person lay a track, placing one step each on individual carpet squares, and then mix up the order of squares (but keeping the same heel-toe orientation so that all the footprints still face the same direction), the dogs can't figure out which direction the track was in, so they're not relying on orientation of footprints.

But if you leave the carpet squares in the same order they were in when the person walked on them, dogs can follow the track in the right direction. Experienced dogs could choose the right direction in as few as five footsteps, which is probably equivalent to just one to two seconds' difference in freshness of the odor between the first and fifth step.

The lesson here? If you're trying to escape from a pack of bloodhounds, don't waste your time trying to backtrack or walk backwards. Run! Preferably, to the nearest airport. 🐾

Can dogs sniff out cancer?

DOGS ARE INFAMOUS FOR sniffing us in embarrassing places. But the next time your dog shows an unusual interest in your body, or even in your bodily wastes, maybe you should pay attention. That's what Trudi's owner did when Trudi showed an unnatural interest in a tiny mole on her leg. The mole turned out to be a melanoma, and thanks to Trudi drawing attention to it, it was removed—whereupon Trudi lost interest.

It was stories like Trudi's that made researchers start to wonder: If dogs can smell miniscule odors, and if diseases and cancers are made up of different kinds of cells that may have their own odors, could dogs detect cancer? They trained two dogs to detect samples with melanoma cells, and found that indeed, the dogs could pick out those samples from among samples with noncancerous cells. So the next time your dog sniffs at a mole, don't ask for his medical degree —it's in his nose. Get to the doctor!

Still, skin cancer is one thing. What about more internalized cancers? Dogs have to be the pee-smelling experts of the world, so why not see if they can detect the presence of bladder cancer in urine samples? When put to the test, trained dogs correctly identified a urine sample from a person with bladder cancer from six noncancerous samples 41 percent of the time. Not perfect, but better than the 14 percent you'd expect by chance. Two dogs were successful 60 percent of the time, and one dog failed miserably. One sample particularly seemed to cause problems—the dogs kept singling it out, even though it was noncancerous. Finally, caution flags went up and doctors sent off for extra tests. Sure enough, the sample-giver had undiagnosed bladder cancer.

Anecdotal evidence exists for dogs finding breast cancer, and research projects are under way to see if they can detect prostate cancer in urine samples and lung cancer in breath samples. In one such project, dogs were between 88 and 97 percent accurate in identifying the breath of people with lung or breast cancer versus cancer-free people. Lung- and breast-cancer patients are known to exhale patterns of biochemical markers in their breath. Who knows? Maybe the day will soon come when you'll be greeted by Dr. Doggy Howser (ouch, sorry) for a dognosis (really, I'll stop!) the next time you go for a checkup. 🐾

Can a dog be scent-blind?

YOU'VE HEARD OF BLIND DOGS AND DEAF DOGS—but can a dog lose its sense of smell? It can happen to people, but it's not as though people rely on their noses to check out their company or decide what to roll in.

But yes, dogs can lose their sense of smell. The technical term is *anosmia*. They can become at least temporarily anosmic, or at least have a reduced sense of smell, from having canine parainfluenza, distemper, head trauma, or being given some corticosteroids. One study found dogs that had recovered from distemper as long as six months earlier were still anosmic. In the case of head trauma, the nerves that lead from the receptors in the nose to the brain can become sheared off where they pass through a mesh of tiny holes in the skull, but fortunately, these are some of the few nerves in the body that can grow back, so the dog can often recover its sense of smell a few months later!

Even though dogs rely so heavily on their smell sense, anosmic dogs don't appear lost or bewildered. In fact, unless they're used for hunting or contraband detection, most owners never even realize anything is amiss. Except for when their dogs quit sniffing so much in those embarrassing places! 🐾

Can dogs recognize seizures before they happen?

PEOPLE WHO SUFFER FROM seizures may have an attack in dangerous situations, making many such people afraid to do scores of the things most people take for granted. If only there was a way to know ahead of time when a seizure was coming....

According to the popular media, there is. Seizure-alert dogs are said to nudge or otherwise alert their owners anywhere from three seconds to forty-five minutes before an imminent seizure. Nobody knows what the dogs are cuing on, although most people assume it's either subtle changes in body language or odor. And without knowing what cues to use for training, it means you can't really train a dog to be a seizure-alert dog—although at least one training center claims to do so by pairing dogs with people who have frequent seizures and rewarding them whenever the person has one—the dogs begin to look for a reward when there's a sign that a seizure is imminent. Most seizure companion dogs are seizure-response dogs, which stay with or assist a person having a seizure by calling 911 or fetching help or medications—all incredibly impressive and potentially life-saving behaviors. But even this is no easy feat; only about 1 out of 100 dogs that start in training graduate. Where's Lassie when you need her?

But people want more, especially since the media hype leads them to expect that a seizure-alert dog can be trained or found with just a little effort. That's misleading. In fact, in a study asking twenty-nine dog owners who had seizures at least once a month, only nine reported that their dogs even stayed with them during a seizure, and only three reported that their dogs alerted them to an impending seizure. Those who had alerting dogs were more likely to have seizures with migraines or auras, and to be closely bonded with their dog. Informal studies have found that while the number of seizure-alert dogs is small, those that do alert to seizures are extremely reliable, maybe as much as 90 percent accurate, with few false alarms.

The take-home message: Don't spend big bucks for a seizure-alert dog, but definitely consider a seizure-response dog—and strive to bond closely with any dog you own. 🐾

How good is a dog's sense of smell?

HERE'S WHAT I DON'T GET: If dogs have such a great sense of smell, why are they always cramming their noses up each other's buttholes? Believe me, you don't need your nose a micrometer away from one to realize this is a dog butt. Not that I've tried. Some things you just know.

But the truth is, the dog is the scenting champion of any animal tested so far, beating out even the most sophisticated scent detection devices on the market. For example, the dog's ability to detect acetic acid, a component of a person's skin secretions, is 10^8 (that is, 100 million) times that of people when tested in laboratory trials. Dogs have been used to sniff out explosives, narcotics, contraband fruits and vegetables, bad catfish, mercury, cows in estrus, cancer, evidence of endangered species, and of course, lost people and criminals.

Why is a dog's nose so much better than our own? The two have the same basic design, but the dog's nose is configured with more of everything. Nasal cavities run the length of the muzzle and contain a labyrinth of curved, delicate bones covered with a layer of mucus and receptor cells (called the *olfactory epithelium*). When a dog is breathing normally, most of the air bypasses the labyrinths and goes right to his lungs. But some of it wafts into the labyrinths, and once he smells something interesting, he starts taking a bunch of small, quick sniffs that direct most of the airflow into the labyrinth part of his nose.

The larger the nasal cavity, the more complex the network of bony scrolls, which allows for a greater area of olfactory epithelium. German Shepherds, for example, have an olfactory area of 170 square centimeters, compared with the Pekingese with only 20 square centimeters. You have a humiliating 4 square centimeters. The greater the olfactory area, the larger the number of olfactory receptors. A German Shepherd has 220 million olfactory receptors, a Dachshund 125 million, and a human only 6 million.

Each of these receptors sends signals to the part of the brain devoted to smell, called the *olfactory bulb*. The olfactory bulb of a person's brain is tiny—smaller than a kernel of corn—and is dwarfed by that of the dog. Sorry guys, but when it comes to smelling, size really does matter, and even the tiniest Chihuahua has an olfactory bulb bigger than yours. 🐾

Do "dog-appeasing pheromones" work?

WOULDN'T IT BE NICE TO press a button and suddenly have your dog calm down? Some scientists think you can, as long as that button releases a dog-appeasing pheromone (DAP) that mimics the smells secreted by lactating dams about three days after birth. Just as newborn puppies find the scent calming, so do adult dogs.

In a study that compared the behavior of shelter dogs constantly exposed to DAP with those not exposed, the DAP-exposed dogs were quieter and more interested in strangers who approached. In another study, dogs that suffered from separation anxiety were given either DAP exposure or a drug (clomipramine) that is regularly prescribed for calming dogs with separation anxiety. The DAP dogs were calmed as much as the dogs given drug therapy. So the next time you shop for air freshener plug-ins, you may want to forget the pine and go for the DAP. 🐾

Why do some dogs chomp and foam at the mouth when they smell the urine of other dogs?

YOU MAY HAVE SEEN YOUR DOG, especially an intact male dog, smell the urine of another dog and even lick at it. As if this weren't enough to gross you out, he then starts chomping his teeth up and down and foaming at the mouth like a rabid dog! Is this just a plan to make sure you never want to kiss him again?

Perhaps, but the main reason is that his mind is not on your kisses, but on the scent of a woman. A doggy woman. A real bitch. This chomping action forces a sample of urine from his mouth up through a tiny passageway in the roof of the mouth that connects the nasal and oral cavities. Within that pathway is a special organ called the *vomeronasal organ*. This organ seems to be specialized for detecting pheromones—chemical messages from other animals of the same species, such as those the female gives off when she is in estrus.

So if you see your dog doing this, don't be alarmed. But if you see your boyfriend doing this, don't let him try to tell you he's just being amorous. The human vomeronasal organ is rudimentary at best. 🐾

Does pepper spray work on dogs?

PEPPER SPRAY WAS ORIGINALLY INTRODUCED in the United States as a dog repellant by, you guessed it, the U.S. Postal Service. It's made from capsicum, a chemical derived from plants in the chili family, which causes extreme inflammation and pain in the eyes and mucous membranes, as well as severe coughing. Its effects last about thirty to forty-five minutes. Single exposure isn't usually harmful to the eyes, but repeated exposure can harm the corneas. A dog that already had breathing or perhaps heart problems could have life-threatening reactions. No records of dog deaths have been reported, but fourteen people have died from pepper spray. So yes, pepper spray may make an aggressive dog think twice, but no, don't use it except in life-threatening emergencies. And be careful—you know what they say about your attacker taking your weapon away and using it against you. 🐾

How good is a dog's eyesight?

IN SOME WAYS, A DOG'S EYESIGHT is better than yours, and in some ways, it's worse. It's better at night. Dog eyes have several features that help them see well in the dark. First, they have large, round corneas—that's the clear part at the front of the eye. They're larger than yours, and collect more light that way. Second, they have larger, rounder lenses within their eyes than yours—also to collect more light. Third, their pupils can widen more than yours, letting in more light. Fourth, they have more rod receptors compared with cone receptors than you do. Not only are rods more sensitive to dim lights, but many rods pool their responses so lots of very dim lights add up to one pretty dim light. Fifth, they have a reflective layer behind the receptors that acts like a mirror, redirecting any light that has passed by the receptors back into them.

In some ways, a dog's eyesight is worse than yours. Everything I just mentioned that makes it better for seeing under dim lighting makes it worse for detecting fine details. It's also not so hot at distinguishing colors, but that's a separate question. 🐾

Can dogs see color, or do they just see in black and white?

YES, DOGS CAN SEE COLOR. No, they don't see colors like you do. Color vision requires the presence of a type of visual receptors called *cones* in the retina of the eye. Most people have three types of cones, each filled with a different type of chemical that maximally absorbs either long wavelength light (red), medium wavelength light (green), or short wavelength light (blue). The colors you see are made up of combinations of all these different cones acting together, sort of like all the tiny dots of your television screen combine to form a full range of color. But some partially color-blind people, most of whom are men, are missing one of the cone types, sometimes the red, but usually the green (they're called *deuteronopes*). All dogs are missing the green cone type, and they have color vision similar to these red-green color-blind people: They see greenish-blue colors as white or gray. They can tell the difference between blues and reds but often confuse hues ranging between greenish-yellow and red. However, it's really impossible to describe what a dog's color world is like, unless you are lucky enough to be a deuteronope yourself...and look (as in "see") like a dog! While discussing dog vision with someone with that problem, I once said as much in jest. It didn't go over very well, so be warned. 🐾

Do dogs' eyes glow when they get angry?

YOU'RE LOST IN THE WOODS, alone at night. You hear growling, so you quickly spin around to shine your flashlight on the danger, only to see a pair of glowing embers blinking back at you. Gulp. A dog—and didn't you hear that a dog's eyes glow when it is angry?

Yes—and no. When a dog is angry, or excited in any way, his pupils automatically dilate (get big). The same thing happens when he's in the dark. And the same thing happens with people. If you shine a light directly into that big pupil, you can get a glimpse of the back of the eye. In a person, the back of the eye is covered with blood vessels, so it just looks red. That's what accounts for red-eye in flash photography. But in a dog, the back of the eye has an extra layer of shiny cells called the *tapetum*. The tapetum isn't there just to look sparkly, or to scare us at night. Its function is to reflect any light that may have slipped past the retinal cells back into the retinal cells for a second chance to be detected. It's one of the reasons dogs have such better night vision than we have. The tapetum lies behind the retina and in front of the blood vessels, so when you shine a light directly into a dog's eye, you see this bright, shining reflection. If you take a flash photo of your dog, you'll see it may be shiny yellow, green, or orange—although a few dog eyes seem to be as red as ours. The color isn't like a mood ring's color; a dog keeps the same color reflection whether he's happy, bored, or angry. 🐾

Can dogs with hair over their eyes see?

OF COURSE THEY CAN SEE—HAIR! All you have to do is flop an equal amount of your own hair in front of your eyes and you'll get the same idea. The closer the strands are to your eye, the larger the gaps between them, so it's not that hard to see. So if the hair's not too thick, you can see pretty well, but at some point it's going to get so thick that all you can see is light and dark. That's why it's really best to tie a dog's hair back out of his eyes. Besides, it's a fashion statement. 🐾

Do dogs need glasses?

INSTEAD OF 20/20 VISION, typical dogs have 20/75 vision, which means that they can just make out details from twenty feet away that a person with good vision can make out at seventy-five feet away.

Would glasses help? In people and dogs alike, the optics of the eye focuses light rays onto the retina in order to get a sharp image. In many people, the light is focused before it even reaches the retina and is unfocused again by the time it gets there, resulting in nearsighted-ness. In others, the light still hasn't come to a focus by the time it reaches the retina, resulting in farsightedness.

It's hard to get a dog to tell you whether "A" or "B", then "1" or "2" is the clearer choice. They get mad and want to bite you, just like you want to bite the optometrist. But you can get a good idea of the eye's focus by looking into the eye with a retinoscope. As far back as 1901, such studies suggested that wild dogs had good focus but most domestic dogs were nearsighted. Modern studies, however, have found that most domestic dogs also have well-focused vision. However, one large study found that certain breeds—German Shepherds, Schnauzers, and especially Rottweilers—tended to be nearsighted, some extremely so. The trait tended to run in families and to be more prevalent in older dogs. So yes, it's possible your dog could need glasses! 🐾

Do old dogs need bifocals?

IF YOU'RE REACHING FOR YOUR GLASSES or holding this book at arm's length, chances are you're over the age of forty. In fact, by the time the average person is thirty-five, he or she is showing signs of *presbyopia—literally*, old vision. It happens because of two things: Your lens constantly grows throughout life, adding layer upon layer, sort of like an onion. Eventually it gets big and stiff, and the little ciliary muscles that attach to the lens and make it change shape start to get weaker. The net result is that your lens can no longer change shape as it needs to in order to accommodate, that is, focus on nearby objects.

What about your dog? The good news is that he suffers very little from this change in the ability to accommodate. The bad news is that he doesn't because he never could do it much in the first place. Even when young, he had the equivalent of presbyopia because his lens is naturally rounder than yours, which makes it more difficult to change its shape, and because his ciliary muscles were weak to start with. So it's not just your old dog that needs bifocals to read; it's your young dog! This is why you shouldn't teach your dog to read; wearing glasses makes him feel self-conscious. 🐾

Do some breeds have better eyesight than others?

WE CAN CREATE BREEDS THAT CAN RUN FASTER, pull harder, bark louder, and do just about anything better than some other breeds. So it stands to reason that we may also have created breeds that can smell, hear, or see better than others. When it comes to seeing, dogs that rely on their eyesight to do their jobs, such as the herding dog that needs to see signals from a distance, the retriever that needs to see downed birds at a distance, or the sighthound that needs to chase fleeing quarry by eyesight wouldn't last if they didn't have acute vision. But is it really better than other dogs'?

Unfortunately, it's hard enough to get good measurements of visual abilities in dogs, much less get them so precise that you could tell the difference between one dog and another. But you can get some clues from the anatomy. There's some evidence that certain breeds tend to have poorer visual focus than others, and some evidence that certain breeds (or at least families within the few breeds tested) have more densely packed photoreceptors than others. Chances are, some breeds do have better vision than others, but as of yet, we don't have any hard evidence for it. 🐾

Can dogs watch TV?

I WAS VISITING A FRIEND when she stuck a videotape in the VCR and said, "Watch this." It was a wildlife program, and her dog glanced at the television screen and then went berserk, rushing the screen and barking whenever a wild animal moved, even with the sound switched off. The dog was perfectly calm when the program showed people (which was reassuring, since I didn't want her starting to eye me like she was eyeing those animals). I left there thoroughly convinced dogs could watch television. But why don't more dogs do it?

A little research revealed that watching television may not be all that easy for dogs. The images on a typical television are refreshed sixty times per second—so often that they appear to be a continuous picture to us. But a dog can detect the flicker of a light that is refreshing as quickly as seventy times per second, suggesting the television image would appear jumpy to him.

Interestingly enough, Maggie's own dogs have shown interest in certain programs and not in others, including shows where one of her dogs actually stalked a silent mountain lion on TV—a revelation that they had seen the local mountain lions up close and personal near her home. The same dog actually tried chasing a dog off screen at one point.

Caroline's dogs, as puppies, were enthralled by videotapes of themselves and littermates, although they found everything else a bore. But as adults, they simply refuse to watch any shows. Maybe they just don't like my choice of programming. Everyone's a critic.

If a dog has his lens removed because of cataracts, should he have a fake one put back in?

IF YOU HAD TO HAVE YOUR LENS removed because of cataracts, you wouldn't dream of walking out of surgery without a fresh artificial lens in the old one's place. Dogs also get cataracts, even when quite young, and need to have their lens removed so they can see. Initially, everyone assumed dogs had such poor vision that they didn't need a replacement lens, but that's not true. Without a lens, instead of 20/75 vision, like the typical dog has, they'd have 20/800 vision. That's bad, but curiously, such dogs still get around pretty well. To correct their vision, they'd need +14 D glasses—try finding those in the store! Human artificial lenses aren't strong enough, but now stronger dog replacement lenses are routinely used when dogs have cataract surgery, giving them much better vision than they had before surgery. But they still can't name those letters on the chart. 🐾

What's a third eyelid?

A THIRD EYELID IS WHAT CLOSES OVER A THIRD EYE. However, if your dog has only two eyes, then a third eyelid is what we commonly call the *nictitating membrane,* a thin tissue that partially closes over the eye from the inner corner of the eye opening. If you pry open your dog' eye while he's sleeping (if he doesn't bite you), you will be able to see it. If he does bite you, well, exactly what did you think would happen? 🐾

Are blind dogs sad?

WHEN PEOPLE LOSE THEIR VISION, they're usually faced with extensive rehabilitation in order to function independently. Not so with dogs. A survey of owners of blind dogs found that most blind dogs still led full and active lives. Most still enjoyed going for walks. Surprisingly, about half of the dogs were taken for walks off leash (except when next to a road), with the owners expressing confidence that the dog was safe. Two dogs were even allowed to roam at will (one was killed by a car). Six owners reported that their dogs could still play ball by relying on their other senses. The dogs could recognize frequent visitors by scent.

The owners did make considerable efforts to contain their dogs in familiar environments. They avoided moving furniture at home or boarding the dog at a kennel. Others posted scent beacons or made carpet runners inside or walkways outside so the dogs could run along them confidently. Despite all such efforts, 12 percent of dogs never learned to adequately cope even in familiar surroundings. Roughly half of the owners reported permanent behavioral or temperament changes in their dogs, mostly in the form of greater timidity, caution, and dependence upon the owner. Dogs would tend to walk rather than run, and some dogs would bark for attention. Dogs that lost their vision relatively suddenly tended to have greater behavioral changes. Unfortunately, none of the dogs ever mastered Braille. What they probably really wanted was their own personal guide dog.

Do dogs need hearing aids?

SOME DOGS MAY GO DEAF FROM OLD AGE, drugs, or exposure to loud noises. Some dogs are deaf in one or both ears from puppyhood. These dogs lose the tiny hair cells and associated structures found inside the ear by about a month after birth, and become deaf. This happens most often in dogs that are mostly white with a few spots, and in some dogs that are mostly white with *merle* (that's a splotched black-and-gray or red-and-tan pattern). The Dalmatian is the best-known spotted example; 20 to 30 percent of this breed are deaf in one or both ears.

By the way, you can test your dog's hearing by standing where he can't see you and saying something he usually responds to. If he doesn't react, stand behind him and whisper, ring a bell, or clap your hands, making sure he can't see you or feel any vibrations or wind currents. He should respond by twitching his ear, turning to look, or if he's panting, stopping so he can hear. A painless test called a brain-stem auditory evoked potential (BAEP) can detect whether signals from the ear are going to the brain, and is considered the definitive canine hearing test.

A hearing aid won't help a deaf Dalmatian or any other dog that has deafness associated with color. And while a hearing aid might help a dog with age-related deafness, dogs are too vain to wear them. One wet dog shake, and the hearing aid is flying across the room and putting somebody's eye out. 🐾

Is it dangerous to live with a deaf dog?

SOME PEOPLE THINK THAT it's too risky to live with a deaf dog because they say the dogs can be easily startled and may for that reason bite. Most people who live with them disagree; after all, you can startle any dog, but you don't expect them to bite you, whether they can hear or not. But you do have to take some precautions with deaf dogs. They can't hear approaching danger, so you must be extra careful with them. They can't hear you call them, so some people who don't realize their dog is deaf think he is stubborn or stupid. Deaf dogs can be trained to recognize hand signals, flashing lights, and vibrations (e.g., thumping the floor or vibrating collars). Books and Internet groups exist that can give owners all sorts of tips. 🐾

Do deaf Dalmatians make better fire dogs because the sirens don't bother them?

NO! WHILE IT'S TRUE THAT Dalmatians are the traditional firehouse dog, and it's true that a higher percentage of Dals are deaf than any other breed, the two facts have nothing to do with one another. For one thing, only about 8 percent of Dalmatians are deaf in both ears (an additional 22 percent are deaf in just one ear), so that means the majority of firehouse Dals hear just fine. For another, Dalmatians came to be associated with firehouses because of their role as coach dogs, where they acted as stylish escorts that kept other dogs from harassing their coach's horses. Later, this job extended to keeping stray dogs away from the horse-drawn fire wagons. Finally, most dogs acclimate to sirens just fine without having to be deaf. Wouldn't it be even less of a good idea to bring a dog to a fire that couldn't even hear you call him out of danger? 🐾

Do silent dog whistles work?

DOG WHISTLES DON'T MIRACULOUSLY command your dog to do things. The idea behind them is that you can make a racket using high-pitched squeals your neighbors can't hear, so you only annoy your dogs and local wildlife. Ideally, dog whistles emit a frequency of between 23,000 and 54,000 Hz, although some emit frequencies as low as 16,000 Hz (which people can hear) or much higher than 55,000 Hz (which dogs can't hear).

You need to train the dog to the "tweet" of the silent whistle just as you would to any verbal command. That said, I once bought a dog whistle and trained and trained my dogs, but they never seemed to be able to learn a thing. Dumb dogs! Except one day, I decided to take it up to an adjoining laboratory that did ultrasound research and that had the equipment to detect the high-pitched sounds dog whistles make. It turned out that this dog whistle wasn't only silent at people-hearing frequencies, but at dog-hearing frequencies as well! Actually, it was silent at bat-hearing frequencies. It was just plain silent. Oh well, what did I expect for $2.98? 🐾

Can dogs hear those ultrasonic pest deterrents?

ULTRASONIC PEST DETERRENTS are supposed to drive rodents out of your home, and the ones mounted on collars are supposed to drive fleas off your dog. The first thing you should know is that they don't work in either case, at least if you are to believe unbiased, controlled scientific studies.

Perhaps that's good, because at least they're not driving your dog away, either—although they may be driving him crazy. These devices typically emit sounds at frequencies of between about 32,000 to 65,000 Hz. So while they're well above the human hearing range, many of them are well within the dog's range, which can detect frequencies of up to 45,000 Hz or higher. And you wonder why he acts crazy? 🐾

Does cropping a dog's ears make him hear better?

AND THE WOLF SAID, "the better to hear you with, my dear..." But do the size and shape of a dog's ear really affect how well he hears? The outer ear acts like a satellite dish, intercepting sound waves and then funneling them into the ear canal. The bigger the ear, the more sound waves it can catch. Ears that prick up into the air overhead can intercept sound waves, and those little convolutions inside the ear act to amplify sounds in certain ways. Although it seems like big, pricked-up ears should best pick up the sound, the only scientific study that tried to answer this question could not find any difference in how well dogs with different types of ears heard. And even if naturally pricked ears did pick up sound better, that doesn't mean cropped ears would, since they lack part of the convolutions within the ear. So, no, cropping a dog's ears does not improve his hearing.

By the way, did you know that dogs have about thirty different sets of muscles for moving the ears, compared with your paltry six sets? 🐾

How do dogs taste their food when they gulp it down so fast?

YOU STARE IN AWE AS THE food goes down in huge gulps. No, it's not your kids or latest dinner date, it's your dog, making you wonder why you ever gave a second thought to what flavor food he'd like best. How can he even taste it?

Well, if you had to eat dog food, wouldn't you try to swallow it whole? Then again, we've seen what dogs eat, so that can't be it. It may be because the dog's strong sense of smell enhances any flavor. The brief time that food passes over the tongue, combined with the odors the dog has already sucked in, may be enough to give gulpers all they want.

By the way, you can slow your dog down by placing an upside-down bowl inside of his regular bowl and sprinkling his food in the space left so he can't get a full mouthful at a time. Gulping can contribute to gas, and sometimes to bloating, so it's well worth discouraging. And who knows—he may discover he actually likes tasting his food! 🐾

Do dogs like artificial sweeteners?

DOES YOUR DOG HAVE A SWEET TOOTH? He may or may not. The appreciation of sweets varies widely among dogs. But if you're thinking of giving him some artificially sweetened foods so you can help him lose weight—well, it might work, because he probably won't touch them. Dogs lack the ability to perceive artificial sweeteners such as saccharin and aspartame as sweet. In fact, they may perceive only saccharin's bitter aftertaste without the sweetness—the worst of both worlds.

Some artificial sweeteners are actually poisonous to dogs—just another reason to skip the sweeteners altogether. 🐾

Does a dog really need his whiskers?

YOUR DOG WOULD BE OFFENDED to hear you call those delicate sensory receptors on his face whiskers, when the real term is *vibrissae*. They're located not just on the muzzle, but on the chin and above each eye. Each is embedded about three times the depth of a normal hair, and has a rich nerve supply. In many show dogs, it's customary to cut them off for a cleaner look. But now that you know they aren't just whiskers, is this clean-shaven look depriving these dogs of an important sense?

A dog's vibrissae function as sensory hairs. Vibrissae contain a mass of erectile tissue with a rich sensory nerve supply. They are similar to human eyelashes that can cause the eye to shut on reflex. Cats with cut vibrissae are less active. And although dogs aren't rats or cats, maps of the canine brain show that a disproportionately large area is devoted to touch sensations from the area of the vibrissae.

Anecdotal evidence with hunting dogs claims that dogs with cut vibrissae tend to come back from a day of hunting with more facial scratches in comparison with those whose vibrissae are intact. That's about the extent of research in dogs. But in rats, cutting the vibrissae interferes with their depth perception, swimming ability, equilibrium, and several other functions that depend on touch.

Try this with your dog: Touch his vibrissae on one cheek, and watch his eye on that side blink. It's as though he had an extra set of eyelashes to warn him that something's coming at his eye. So if you're ever tempted to see how your dog would look without whiskers, cut your own eyelashes off at the same time and see how you like it. 🐾

Why are puppies born with their eyes closed?

BECAUSE THEY'RE AFRAID OF WHAT they might see? Actually, all *altricial* animals (animals born relatively helpless, such as carnivores) have closed lids at birth. Their visual system is still immature and the eyes won't open until about ten to fourteen days of age—although they can still respond to light.

During the fetal development of all mammals, the eyelids grow together and temporarily fuse closed over the eyes. Animals, such as those with hooves, that need to stand up on their feet and get going soon after birth, are born at a more mature stage, and their lids have already opened by the time they're born. Humans, too, have lids that are fused while in the womb but that will have opened by the time of birth. Puppies and many other mammals, however, still have their lids fused together at birth.

Some puppies can get eye infections beneath the closed lids. The areas start bulging with discharge that can't get out. A veterinarian can treat this by, among other things, partially opening the lids so that medications can gain access to the eye. Opening the lids early does not seem to hurt the dog's later vision. But don't try this at home! 🐾

Can newborn puppies see, hear, smell, or taste?

NEWBORN PUPPIES ARE BORN with less mature nervous systems than newborn humans, but they can still sense much of the world around them. A newborn can smell well enough to move toward the scent of her own mother, and can either smell or taste well enough to prefer a teat that has her own or her mother's saliva on it. Her taste buds are already mature but won't be adultlike until she's ten days old. She has definite taste preferences and already can tell sweet from nonsweet.

She can't regulate her body temperature, but she senses when she's too hot or cold. If she's too cold, she swings her head back and forth until her muzzle touches something, then crawls toward it. If she's too hot, she turns away from anything touching her. She feels pain, and cries and pulls away if something is hurting her, although her reflexes are still slow.

Light penetrates her closed lids, and by four days of age, she even "blinks" (flinches) when it's really bright. When the lids open, at about ten to fourteen days, her vision will be blurry because the eye is not mature. In fact, she'll be five weeks old before it's nearly adult-like and ten weeks old before it's completely mature.

Her ear canals are also closed and won't open until about fifteen days of age. She can definitely hear by two weeks of age, but her hearing won't be adultlike until three weeks later. 🐾

Can puppies smell in the womb?

THE SENSE OF SMELL IS ONE of the first that newborn pups use to locate their dam's teats. If it's present at birth, what about before birth? The answer is, yes. Researchers added a flavor to a pregnant dog's diet that caused her amniotic fluid to take on a particular odor. When these puppies were born, they sought this smell over other smells, suggesting that newborns may recognize the scent of their mother from prenatal exposure to her scent. 🐾

6

THE
SEXUAL DOG

Can dogs be homosexual?

DON'T TELL YOUR ROTTWEILER, but yes, chances are, dogs can be bisexual. Researchers have found examples in more than 450 species, including dogs, of some sort of same-sex sexual, courting, or other behavior commonly thought of as homosexual. Some male dogs have been reported to ignore females in estrus in preference to spending time with a favored male friend, but more often, dogs act more bisexual, taking sex and courtship wherever they can find it. Instances have been reported of male dogs having anal sex with other male dogs, but in none of those cases has the recipient been labeled as willing! Perhaps more often, playful or dominant mounting behavior happened to accidentally hit the mark. Males around females in estrus sometimes mount each other in frustration. Multiple-male households can have mounting "trains" in that case, with one male on the back of another, which is on another, and so on. Bitches in estrus and during false pregnancies often take turns mounting one another, thrusting as enthusiastically as any male.

Don't mistake mounting behavior in puppies and in play with homosexual behavior. Mounting, whether by or on a male or female, is a normal dominance role-playing behavior in both puppies and adults.

Do dogs get stuck when having intercourse?

YOU MAY HAVE SEEN A COUPLE of young canine lovers by the roadside who seem to suddenly realize their public display of affection is inappropriate. Don Juan jumps off, the couple look like they're ready to split and head their separate ways, but there's a problem: they're stuck. Should you really blow your horn? Throw water on them? Call the fire department?

Call animal control, maybe, since one of them is going to be having puppies in two months. But being stuck, or tied, is perfectly normal for dogs. That's because a dog's penis is a multitalented thing. Just as with the human penis, the dog's penis engorges with blood, enlarging greatly and stiffening so that it can penetrate the female's vulva. Once inside, two things happen: The male ejaculates, and a unique part of his penis, the *bulbous glandis* (or bulb), further engorges with blood, enlarging so much that the penis becomes locked within the vagina in an involuntary sexual embrace.

It's normal for the male to dismount once he's ejaculated the sperm-rich fraction of his semen. The area of the penis behind the bulb doesn't fill with as much blood as the rest of it, so it's able to twist 180 degrees without hurting the dog. The male will usually turn around, his face pointing in the opposite direction as the female, looking for all the world like this was a big mistake. During this time, though, something important is happening. The male continues to ejaculate small streams of prostatic fluid, which help propel the earlier sperm-rich fraction up toward her eggs. A tie normally lasts from ten to forty-five minutes, but can last for over an hour. Eat your heart out, guys!

By the way, if you find your dogs tied, and puppies were not on your agenda for the future, it's too late. The length of the tie appears to have no bearing on how many puppies are born, or whether or not a bitch gets impregnated. In fact, plenty of litters have been born with so-called outside ties, in which the male ejaculated while the bulb was still outside the female. 🐾

Can a litter have more than one father?

"I HAVE TWO DADDIES." That's what some puppies, or at least litters, can say these days. Some can even claim three daddies. In cases where females have been spotted being less than selective with their lovers, it's long been suspected that puppies in the same litter could have more than one sire. Not only has DNA testing proved that, but it's made it possible to purposefully mate a female to more than one stud, DNA-test the puppies, and register them with different parents. Why would anyone want to do that? In breeds where homes are hard to find, especially when they have large litters, it's one way to maintain genetic diversity without the breed risking overpopulation.

Some people object on moral grounds, but even though her doggy friends may call her slutty, most she dogs don't seem to object to mating with more than one stud. But if that's a dilemma, you can always use artificial insemination to impregnate her. But a word of caution: Recent findings have suggested that whichever male's sperm gets there first tends to sire most of the puppies. So before you call "come and get it!" be sure you've decided who gets to go first. Or better yet, mix the sperm together and do it artificially. And be forewarned that a multiple-sired litter is going to cost you a lot more for DNA testing and American Kennel Club (AKC) registration.

Is there such a thing as a doggy paternity test?

THE TWO SNARLED AT EACH OTHER, typical Jerry Springer guests, as the envelope carrying the paternity test results were brought in. They would decide which one was the father of the pup that, if he could realize what was happening, would pray he was switched at birth. Some weeks earlier, cheek-swab samples were collected from each dog and submitted for DNA profiling....

DNA parentage testing makes matters dicey not only for studs that may wish to shirk their fatherly responsibilities, but for the less than scrupulous breeders out there: AKC can randomly inspect large-scale breeding operations to determine whether their pedigrees are accurate, by comparing what pedigrees claim and DNA disclaims.

DNA testing also allows the AKC to respond to complaints of suspicions that parents or sires are not as alleged. Does that puppy you paid big money for resemble the breeder's pet bitch more than their top-winning bitch? Did your bitch whelp a litter that looks more like the stud owner's oversexed youngster than his older dog? Now you can demand to know the truth. But it will cost you if you're wrong: To discourage frivolous allegations, a written complaint and $500 deposit (returned if the charges are validated) must be submitted by the complainant.

Here's how it works: The DNA profile is a collection of genetic markers (segments of DNA that have many different forms in the dog population, and that are reliably passed from parent to offspring). Each parent has a pair of possible markers at each marker location, and each parent randomly contributes a copy of one of those markers to each offspring. This means that each puppy also has a pair of markers, one inherited from the sire and one from the dam, at each location.

One marker can easily be traced to the dam; either the remaining marker must match one of the proposed sires, or that male is unlikely to be the sire. Say the dam's markers at one location are AB, and the sire's are BC. Puppy #1 is AB, puppy #2 is BB, and puppy #3 is BD. Puppies 1 and 2 could have been sired by that sire, but puppy #3 could not have been because the sire had no D marker to contribute. At least two nonmatching markers must be present of the fourteen routinely tested in order for the AKC to exclude a dog as a possible sire. Paternity testing is now fairly routinely performed in dogs to see which one is the sire of an accidental or a multiple-sired litter. But even when they're fingered, getting them to pay pup support is still next to impossible. 🐾

Can DNA tests tell one breed from another?

SEVERAL YEARS AGO, nobody thought you could ever tell one breed from another through its DNA, but scientists have recently found that, using *microsatellite markers* (which are segments of DNA that vary greatly among different dogs but tend to be the same in closely related individuals), they could assign distinct microsatellite "signatures" to breeds. These signatures are so distinct that 99 percent of purebred dogs they've tested so far can be assigned to their correct breeds based on their DNA. Only four breeds—the Chihuahua, Presa Canario, German Shorthaired Pointer, and Australian Shepherd—of the eighty-five they have tested failed to form distinct breed signature DNA groups.

Several breeds do have very similar signatures to other breeds. Close pairs include the Alaskan Malamute and Siberian Husky; Collie and Shetland Sheepdog; Greyhound and Whippet; Bernese Mountain Dog and Greater Swiss Mountain Dog; Mastiff and Bullmastiff; and West Highland White Terrier and Cairn Terrier; so close as to be indistinguishable as are the Belgian Tervuren and Belgian Sheepdog. At present, DNA testing can't be used to definitively say whether a dog is a pure or mixed breed. But this sort of information can be valuable in forensic investigations, where dog DNA has already often played a role in convicting the bad guys. 🐾

Can dogs be identical twins?

MOST DOGS ARE BORN AS PARTS OF LITTERS, so in that sense, they're often fraternal twins, triplets, or—what's the word for ten? Dectuplets? Or maybe just tenpuplets...But few verified cases of identical twins in dogs exist. Once in a while you'll hear a claim that littermates are identical twins because they look alike, or have identical markings, but that's not sufficient evidence. Identical twins come from the same fertilized egg, which splits and becomes two separate embryos. Depending on when the split occurs, the twins may share a placenta (the later the split, the greater the chance they will share one placenta), but not always. Some dog breeders have reported puppies being born with only one placenta between them, but there's always a chance that two puppies are born one after another and that one placenta has become detached and only been delivered later. It's also possible two placentas can grow together and appear to be a single entity. DNA tests are the only conclusive way to prove identical twin dogs, and no reports exist of dogs proven to be genetically identical. By the way, identical twins would not necessarily share the same markings, since certain characteristics, such as the size and placement of spots, are determined during in utero development by random cell splits.

Can dogs be conjoined, like Siamese twins?

REPORTS OF CONJOINED KITTENS ARE UNUSUAL, but not rare. Reports of conjoined puppies, however, are extremely rare. (And no, dogs tied while mating don't count!) Some dogs have been reported with stubs of additional legs, but true conjoined dogs would not live long and probably tend to be discarded rather than reported. Conjoined twins usually result from an incomplete split of a fertilized egg that would have produced identical twins. Perhaps dogs simply have very few cases of identical twinning and, as a result, few conjoined twins.

If a female is bred near the start of her receptive time and again near the end, a week later, will some puppies be born a week premature?

YOUR DOG HAS A LITTER OF PUPPIES, all plump and healthy, except one is much smaller than the others and seems slower to develop. You think back and recall that the stud dog repeatedly bred with her over almost a week while she stood for him. Could the runt have been conceived well after the rest of the puppies?

I've known breeders who refused to allow dogs to mate for the full period of the female's receptive period to avoid just such cases. When the female comes into season, she's receptive only for a period of four to eight days, even though she's technically in season for about three weeks. Only during her receptive phase will she allow males to breed with her. At the end of this phase, she'll ovulate.

What's important to realize is that she's not ovulating throughout this phase. Ovulation of all her eggs occurs within forty-eight hours. Sperm can stay alive in her reproductive tract for many days, probably as long as a week, so sperm isn't wasted from matings occurring well before ovulation. In fact, some recent research indicates that sperm cells just park themselves along the walls of the reproductive tract and wait not only for ovulation, but for the eggs to mature enough to be ready for fertilization. Then they all rush in at once and race to be the chosen one. So at most, fetuses may differ in age by a day or two, and more likely, not even by that much. Runts are more likely caused by bad luck in relation to where that particular puppy embryo was implanted, happening to find a place that didn't get as much nourishment as others. Once the runt bellies up to the nursing bar, he'll probably catch up.

Can big dogs have sex with little dogs?

THINK ABOUT IT: Do you really think a Chihuahua male can reach high enough to get his little arms around his beloved Irish Wolfhound female? And while well-endowed for his size, even a Chihuahua's penis has its limits. Sure, we've all heard stories about the female who laid on the ground so the male could reach her, but that's not the normal mating position, and none of these stories has been documented. Conversely, if an Irish Wolfhound male tried to mount a Chihuahua female, with the first thrust he'd send her flying out behind him like a center hiking a football. There's no way, short of her standing on a table (and that wouldn't work either), that he's going to get things lined up. Which is lucky, because even though her vulva does greatly expand when she's in estrus, there are limits, and it doesn't get any longer in there, and, well, things could get ugly. 🐾

Is it dangerous to breed a little female to a much bigger male because the fetus will get too big?

IT'S COMMONLY ASSUMED THAT breeding a big male to a little female is a recipe for killing the female by means of a fetus that grows so big she just bursts. Fortunately, physical barriers make breeding between dogs of extremely different sizes unlikely, at least without human help or artificial insemination. Also fortunately, it turns out that the size of the dam puts a limit on how large the fetus can grow. A fetus from a large male and small female will be similar in size to whatever is the norm for females of that size to whelp. After birth, the puppy will grow more rapidly to reach its genetically determined size. 🐾

Can dogs mate with wolves, coyotes, or foxes?

DOGS, WOLVES, COYOTES, AND JACKALS can all mate with one another and produce viable and fertile offspring—although jackals are somewhat picky and will mate with domestic dogs only if they've been raised with them. However, none of them can produce viable offspring when mated to a fox. That's because while dogs, wolves, coyotes, and jackals share the same number and arrangement of chromosomes, foxes do not. So if somebody claims they have an animal that is part fox, part dog—they don't. 🐾

Do dogs get sexually transmitted diseases?

THE MOOD IS SET, THE TIME IS RIGHT. He nuzzles her ear, makes his move. Then comes those romance-ruining words: "What about STDs?" Dogs don't wear condoms, so safe sex depends on having owners with sex education. Fortunately, syphilis, gonorrhea, chlamydia, and HIV don't afflict dogs. But they can fall victim to other sexually transmitted diseases (STDs).

One such disease is canine transmissible venereal tumor (CTVT), which made medical history when it was identified as the first known instance of tumor cells being passed from one animal to another. While we normally think of a cancer as an individual's own cells that have run amok, CTVT is more like a clone colony of some parasite that has found a way to skip from dog to dog. Rather than matching the DNA of its host dog, CTVT even has a different number of chromosomes than dogs do, and is genetically almost identical in every dog. Although CTVT is most commonly spread by mating, it can also be spread by touching, licking, or sniffing existing tumors.

CTVT sounds scary, but the STD that strikes fear into the heart of dog breeders is brucellosis. It can be transmitted sexually or by any mucous membrane coming into contact with infected substances such as aborted fetuses, uterine discharge, milk, urine, and saliva. When one dog in a household or kennel is infected, this bacterial disease can run rampant and infect every other dog in close proximity. Fortunately, there's a test for it, and all dogs should be tested within three weeks prior to breeding.

Then there's canine herpes, which sounds like a definite STD. It can be spread by breeding, but more often is spread through saliva and nasal secretions. Most canines that go to dog parks or shows have been exposed to herpes. Unfortunately, if a bitch is pregnant, her puppies can be resorbed, aborted, or born with herpes. Puppies under three weeks of age die typically because they cannot mount a fever, which is necessary to kill the herpes virus. If herpes is confirmed in a litter (easily done by a quick autopsy of a refrigerated, not frozen, puppy), surviving pups can be saved by placing them in incubators.

Just as with people, STDs can strike anyone, even nice dogs from nice families. 🐾

Can a woman get pregnant from a dog?

OBVIOUSLY, THIS QUESTION BRINGS UP even more questions of a delicate nature—about bestiality. So let's not pussyfoot around. Male dogs can have sex with female humans (and anal sex with male humans). It is not something they do naturally, but, for whatever reason, people can induce and train them to do so. And depending on size, they can even achieve a tie—which reports claim can be rather uncomfortable. In fact, stories abound of people, with large dogs attached, calling for medical assistance when they found themselves tied and apparently panicked. Now, personally, I think if your biggest worry is whether you can get pregnant from engaging in this practice, then I don't know what to say except that, worry not, you can't get pregnant from a dog, for a number of reasons, including the fact that the egg and sperm are not compatible, and that the chromosome sizes, organization, and number are totally different. And, you're also not going to catch an STD from each other. You may end up being arrested, since such practice is considered animal cruelty and is illegal in some states. You know, getting a date with a human really isn't all that difficult.... 🐾

Can a dog get pregnant from a man?

HUMAN MALES HAVE BEEN FALLING in lust with animals of other species for centuries, including those that can only be described as real dogs. Because a female dog's vulva is very small unless she is in estrus, the only time it is possible for a man to have sex with a dog is when she is in season, and then, only if she is a large dog.

Now, far be it from me to be judgmental, but for you perverts who are worried that you may have to pay pup support for Jo-Jo the dog-faced boy, fear not: It is impossible for human sperm to fertilize dog eggs. It is possible for you to get arrested, however, and bitten—possibly in a delicate area. 🐾

Can giving a pregnant dog calcium end up killing her?

MAKING AND NURSING PUPPIES REQUIRES a lot of calcium on the part of the dam, so it only makes sense to supplement her diet with calcium during her pregnancy, right? Wrong! Doing so actually increases her chance of a potentially fatal condition called eclampsia.

That's because the body's production of calcium, and its ability to take calcium from its own bones when needed, is regulated by a secretion called the *parathyroid hormone*. When she gets plenty of calcium in her diet, her body's production of parathyroid hormone greatly decreases. That's usually fine when she's still pregnant, but once she has puppies and they begin to nurse a lot, she suddenly needs large amounts of calcium to make enough milk—and now she doesn't have enough parathyroid hormone to remove calcium from her bones. Instead, her blood calcium levels plummet, and this causes serious neurological problems, even death. What seemed like a good idea has ended up sending many dogs, especially toy breed dams, to the emergency vet. Don't do it! 🐾

Do some breeds need Caesarean sections?

MOST DOGS BELIEVE IN NATURAL CHILDBIRTH, but members of some breeds opt for more modern methods. Small breeds are more likely to require C-sections, and *brachycephalic* animals (that's the fancy word for dogs with squished-in faces) are so likely to need them that it's safer to simply plan one ahead of time. These dogs tend to have large heads compared with their dam's pelvic opening, and they're often too large to fit. Once stuck part way, the dam can become exhausted trying to expel them, and the uterine contractions can injure the puppy or even cause the uterus to rupture.

Incidentally, C-sections are also often needed in the case of single-ton litters. When only one puppy is present, it tends to grow larger, making whelping more difficult. In addition, puppies produce a hormone that stimulates the whelping process, and it's likely that a single puppy doesn't produce enough to get things rolling. By the time the breeder figures out the bun's been in the oven too long, it may be a dicey situation.

In either case, an emergency C-section is often needed to save the lives of stuck or reluctant puppies and their dams. A planned Caesarean is much safer, cheaper, and easier on everyone. Progesterone testing while breeding can pinpoint her exact day of ovulation, so you know exactly how long the puppies have been baking and you can take them out of the oven at just the right time. 🐾

Why do some dogs think they're pregnant when they're not?

YOU'VE GUARDED YOUR INTACT FEMALE during her season as though she were a damsel confined in a castle tower, fending away amorous Romeos. You swear nobody got to her. But—gulp—why is she looking like a walking dairy bar? And now she even seems to be going into labor! But where are the puppies?

Sometimes, the puppies are there in the form of stuffed animals and other toys. Females in false pregnancies often become engorged with milk, adopt toys as their puppies, and may even go into a false labor. But they're not pregnant. Don't worry, your dog isn't mentally ill, or ill at all. She, like 87 percent of all intact female dogs, is experiencing a false or pseudopregnancy. In fact, all nonpregnant bitches have some degree of false pregnancy, usually accompanied by increased mammary development, between six and twenty weeks following estrus. Some even exhibit an enlarged abdomen, nesting behavior, decreased activity, aggression, maternal behavior, and even labor, complete with abdominal contractions. The more convincing cases cause household accusations of "Who let the dog out?"

This realistic charade occurs because intact bitches undergo the same hormonal changes following estrus whether they're pregnant or not. First, progesterone levels remain elevated until right before the anticipated whelping date, even in nonpregnant females. When progesterone levels drop, it stimulates both birth and milk production (which is also controlled by prolactin). Many females that are spayed right after they come out of season often have a false pregnancy because spaying causes a drop in progesterone.

False pregnancies will usually run their course in two to four weeks, but they can sometimes cause mammary discomfort or even mastitis. Some bitches even nurse from themselves, which stimulates even more milk production. Cutting down on her food and making sure the mammary glands aren't stimulated can sometimes decrease milk production, but be sure it really is a false pregnancy. We once knew somebody who returned home from the veterinarian with a diagnosis of false pregnancy and delivered the news to his disbelieving wife. After a long debate, the wife won the argument by pointing to the dog and saying, "If she's not pregnant, then what is that on the floor?" It was the first of seven real, not pseudopuppies! 🐾

Can dogs be cloned?

WHEN SNUPPY (short for Seoul National University puppy) made history as the world's first living cloned dog, dog owners couldn't help but wonder if they'd found a way to keep their dog by their side forever. Short of taxidermy, probably not.

That was the dream behind the Missyplicity Project, started in 1997 at Genetic Savings & Clone with funding from a wealthy owner who yearned to clone his beloved husky mix, Missy. But after ten years and $19 million invested, researchers there finally admitted defeat. It's not that they're inept; they were able to clone a cat on the second attempt, back in 2002. It's just that dog reproductive physiology makes dog cloning the most difficult of any mammal attempted.

Here's why: To clone a mammal, you start with harvested mature eggs. But because dogs ovulate only twice a year, and scientists haven't found a way to induce canine ovulation, eggs can be hard to come by. And, unlike in other mammals, in which eggs mature in the ovaries, dog eggs mature in the oviducts about seventy-two hours after ovulation. So instead of aspirating (sucking out) eggs fairly easily from the ovaries, they must be surgically removed from the tiny oviduct. After removal, the eggs' genetic material is replaced with that of the animal to be cloned. In other mammals, the resulting embryos are grown in the laboratory for several days and then implanted into surrogate mothers that have been given hormones to prepare them for pregnancy. But nobody has ever been able to grow dog embryos outside of a dog. So as soon as the eggs begin to develop into embryos—within four hours of starting the cloning process—they must be surgically placed back into the oviduct. And because no hormones have ever been found that prepare dogs for pregnancy, the eggs must be implanted back into the same dog from which they were just removed.

The South Korean researchers implanted 1,095 eggs in 123 dogs, resulting in only three pregnancies, with two surviving to birth. One pup died of pneumonia; the other, Snuppy, is doing fine. Snuppy is an exact genetic match of his three-year old-genetic donor, an Afghan Hound named Tai. Since then, they've cloned two female Afghan Hounds.

With one company now charging $150,000 to produce each puppy, cloning doesn't seem to present much of a threat to a world inundated with canine reruns. Besides, can you imagine the anarchy that would result if famous show dogs were ever cloned? Entire show rings would be filled with identical dogs. Maybe that's one reason the AKC won't register clones. 🐾

Would a cloned dog be just like the original dog?

CLONED ANIMALS HAVE THE SAME DNA as their donors, but—just as identical twins aren't exactly identical—cloned dogs wouldn't be exactly identical. That's because of a couple of factors. First, environment plays a big role. If you cloned your favorite dog, you'd probably figure the second one would turn out better because you'd know what behavior problems you could nip in the bud, for example. You'd be a different owner, very likely with a different family, and your new dog would have different experiences.

Even physical traits wouldn't be absolutely identical. For example, many people were surprised when the first cloned cat had spots that didn't match its donor. That's because the size and placement of spots is somewhat of a chancy matter (although being spotted versus nonspotted is the result of genes). During development of a spotted dog, some cells almost randomly develop pigment, and then when these cells divide, all the cells derived from them will be spotted. But the placement of those spots depends on just where that first pigmented cell was located, and the extent of them depends on how early in development it became spotted and how many offspring cells spread from it.

So while cloning might get you the next best thing to your original, it won't be exactly alike. Vive la différence! 🐾

7

DOG CARE

Why do dogs drink from toilets?

SOME DOGS HAVE WHAT can only be called a "potty mouth." They run into the bathroom every time someone leaves the toilet lid up and then start drinking. Ick. But why do they do that?

Well, there are several possible reasons why. The first is that it's a readily available water source that is constantly refilling. If your dog's water bowl is out, he may figure it's as good of a watering hole as anything else. Second, your dog may be telling you something about the quality of the water you're putting in the bowl. For one thing, water from the toilet tends to be a bit fresher. The porcelain provides a natural way to cool the water, thus making it more appealing on a hot day.

You can stop your dog from drinking from the toilet by keeping the lid and the door to the bathroom closed. You can further make your dog happy by giving him water from one of those recycling pet fountains.

Why do dogs have doggy breath?

YOU KNOW WHAT I'M TALKING ABOUT. Your dog comes up and plants a big wet slurpy kiss right on you, but ugh, why doesn't he get a breath mint? Why are dogs' breath, well, doggy?

You may be surprised to learn that doggy breath isn't natural. It's a sign of gum disease called gingivitis—yeah, the same stuff that attacks your gums. If your dog has bad breath, the reason is that he has a mouth problem and needs to see a veterinarian to at least clean his teeth.

You can avoid doggy breath by brushing your dog's teeth at least twice a week. (More often is preferable.)

But all bets are off if he's been eating doggy doo.

Why can dogs eat garbage and not get sick?

GARBAGE GUTS. You've seen dogs eat garbage all the time and not get the least bit sick. So, how do they manage it?

The truth is that while dog evolution allowed for more or less chowing down on anything that presented itself in human trash pits, dogs are susceptible to getting sick on garbage and icky stuff, just like we are. They can get sick from *E. coli*, salmonella, and campylobacter poisoning, just as we do. What's more, bones and other sharp objects in garbage can hurt a dog. Just because he's gotten lucky in the past doesn't mean he'll be lucky in the future. So, keep your garbage away from your dog—and both of you will be the better for it.

Can you change a dog's name?

YOU'VE JUST ADOPTED A DOG. The problem is, someone already gave him the name "Rover"—which you're none too keen about. Can you change your dog's name without any serious repercussions?

Well, believe it or not, your new dog doesn't care whether you call him Rover or Duke or Rusty—as long as you don't call him late for dinner. He's happy to hang out with you whatever you call him. Case in point: Maggie has changed the names of many of her dogs after adopting them. In some cases, a change of name even appeared to be welcomed by the dog.

Can an older dog bond with someone?

WHEN PEOPLE THINK ABOUT GETTING a dog, they think primarily about getting a puppy. After all, a puppy is cute and will bond with the new owner. But what about older dogs? Do they bond with their owners too?

The answer is a resounding "Yes!" Because dogs are bred to be like juvenile wolves (a trait called *neoteny*), an older dog can bond just as well as a puppy to an owner, if the owner spends enough time with him. Maggie has owned many adult dogs that bonded to her just as well as puppies. So, don't overlook the older dogs when looking for a pet. 🐾

Are eggs good for a dog's coat?

EGGS ARE, WITHOUT A DOUBT, a pretty healthy food when it comes to dogs. They're a great protein source and have plenty of vitamins and cholesterol to make for a shiny coat. (Dogs don't suffer from clogged arteries like we do.) But like anything, there are caveats to the egg lore. For one thing, cooked, whole eggs are better for the dog, and only once a week or so as a treat. Raw egg whites tie up the vitamin biotin, thus causing a biotin deficiency if fed to dogs (and people!). Raw eggs can also carry salmonella, which can cause both you and your dog to get sick. Likewise, making eggs a large portion of your dog's diet can cause some nutritional imbalances. So, everything in moderation. 🐾

Are table scraps OK?

MY DAD USED TO TELL ME how they fed their dogs table scraps as main meals when they were pups. In fact, even now people love giving their dogs table scraps. But should you?

Well, within moderation. Table scraps are often the inedible portions of meat and vegetables that can be pretty tasty to dogs. Problem is, table scraps are low in vitamins and usually loaded with calories, high in fat, sugar, and salt—things your dog really doesn't need. So feeding your dog all or a large portion of table scraps as its meal is a bad idea.

However, many veterinary nutritionists recommend that if you have to give your dog treats, you should try cooked vegetables (no onions) or cuts of lean meat and make sure that the percentage is no more than 5 percent of your dog's total caloric intake for the day. That way, your dog can enjoy tidbits and still remain healthy.

One study found that dogs that were given table scraps as part of their diet actually had a lower frequency of bloating. 🐾

Is alcohol OK for a dog?

SOME DOGS, LIKE PEOPLE, like the taste of alcohol, most notably beer. So, one has to wonder if it's OK to let your dog imbibe while you do.

In a word, no.

Alcohol is technically a poison that can kill you, especially if you have too much. For many people who have a drink or two, it's not a big deal because the amount of alcohol is usually appropriate for their body weight. However, with dogs, it's a different story.

People usually weigh somewhere between 100 and 200 pounds. Most dogs don't weigh even 100 pounds soaking wet, so alcohol will affect them far faster than a person—they hardly need much at all to get drunk. But the real problem is alcohol poisoning. Even a little beer can kill a dog, so a human-sized portion is dangerous. What's more, grapes can cause renal failure in dogs, so wine is definitely out.

So, when having a wine and cheese party with your pooch, skip the wine and choose the cheese. 🐾

Why do some dogs hate car rides and others love them?

AH, TO FEEL THE WIND IN ONE'S FACE and take off for the open road! Some dogs love riding in cars, but other dogs are positively catatonic when approaching said vehicle. What gives?

Most dogs that love riding in the car have associated good things with it. They go to places like the park and places where they can do fun activities. But what about the dogs that hate car rides? There are several reasons for this aversion. The first is that the dog may suffer from carsickness just like a person (hint: a vet can help you with that). The second reason is that the dog associates riding in the car with traumatic events such as trips to the vet, trips to the boarding kennel, leaving his mom, etc. Let's face it, you wouldn't be thrilled with the car if all it did was take you to the doctor to be poked and prodded. Third, some dogs just don't like the smell and sound of the car. It's noisy and gives off several unpleasant odors (just like Uncle Bob, huh?). A trainer can help your dog get over his dislike of cars. 🐾

If a dog kills another animal, is that dog too dangerous to own?

THIS LINE OF THOUGHT HAS BEEN around for ages. Maggie remembers hearing how a dog that killed another animal was put down because it was purportedly aggressive. But is it really? And do you have anything to worry about if your dog kills a squirrel or rabbit? Not likely.

Dogs are predators. Dogs evolved from the wolf, which means that within them, there's still the instinct to hunt. This very instinct enables the herding dogs to do what they do—"hunt" the sheep without biting them—and enables many other dogs to do the tasks they were bred to do.

When a dog hunts a squirrel or a rabbit, that creature incites what is called the "prey drive." The dog knows this isn't a person—it's food. The dog doesn't necessarily associate the rabbit with other dogs or people.

The caveat is whether the dog marks people as prey. This can occur through training, poor breeding, or poor socialization. Or it might be a case of mistaken identity. Regardless, it is essentially a breakdown in the dog-human relationship and may or may not have anything to do with whether a dog is truly dangerous or aggressive. 🐾

Does tomato juice work on skunk odor with dogs?

AH, THE AGE-OLD QUESTION: Does tomato juice work on skunk odor? Well, despite what you might have seen on old sitcoms, the answer is most positively "no!"

You see, skunk odor is a mixture of oils and some stinky compounds called *thiols*. It's squirted from glands on either side of the skunk's anus (you wanted to know that, didn't you?). Skunks squirt when alarmed, and usually when a dog tries to chase them. So when a dog is skunked, what do you do?

Well, let's look at the reason why tomato juice doesn't work. The thiols—which give off the same stench that comes from decayed bodies, rotten food, and poop—make up the smell. Tomato juice does nothing in its composition to counteract the smell. But what happens, interestingly enough, is that your nose gets overloaded because of the smell and after a bit, you get desensitized. It starts smelling less bad because you've grown used to it. Sad but true.

Surprisingly, there's a homemade remedy that works really well. A chemist by the name of Paul Krebaum came up with this solution to chemically combat skunk odor. It consists of:

1 quart 3% hydrogen peroxide (fresh bottle)
¼ cup baking soda (sodium bicarbonate)
1 to 2 teaspoons liquid dish soap

You must mix it up at once and use it. Don't save any and don't store it in a closed container because it will explode. Don't get any in your dog's eyes, and rinse it off really well with water. Works like a charm. Maggie knows from firsthand experience. 🐾

Why do dogs prefer cat food?

YOU SET OUT A BOWL OF YOUR DOG'S food and then go to feed the cat. Your dog decides that the cat food is far more tasty—what's going on?

Well, there are several factors at work here. The first is that cat food is higher in protein than dog food, and your dog is naturally attracted to higher protein/higher fat foods. Second, cats tend to be a bit picky when it comes to food, so cat food is a bit more aromatic to entice the feline—and thus entices your dog. Lastly, your dog is not above a game of one-upmanship. He likes to steal the cat's food because it's there and because he knows it'll annoy the cat.

Naturally, dogs shouldn't eat cat food. You don't want a catty dog, now do you? 🐾

Can dogs die from eating onions?

A FEW YEARS AGO I was on an e-mail group, and one of the folks there posted a note that said how funny it was that her two Jack Russell Terriers had just gotten into her pantry and eaten a ten-pound bag of onions. Everyone was laughing, it seemed, but me. It wasn't just the threat of a possible case of doggy breath or massive deadly gas attack that might destroy her county, but that her dogs could die from eating onions. I immediately asked if she was exaggerating, or was really sure they'd eaten that much. When she assured me that they had, I told her to call her emergency vet right now. In one of the rare cases of somebody actually believing me, she did. It's probably what saved her dogs' lives.

Within a few hours, both dogs were peeing brown urine, and one dog had white gums and could no longer stand. The brown urine was the waste product from hemolyzed (that is, broken up) red blood cells. Onions contain a chemical that hemolyzes dogs' red blood cells. The sicker of the two dogs, which probably ate more onions, had white gums because he had so few red blood cells left. He was, in essence, bleeding to death without a cut. After a blood transfusion and a week in the hospital he was able to walk out, weak but on his way to recovery, probably ready to tackle another bag of onions. I doubt he'll find any around his house.

You don't have to freak out if your dog eats an onion slice. But use common sense unless you want the bag of onions you leave on the pantry floor to be the most expensive vegetable you ever buy. 🐾

Is pork bad for dogs?

"DON'T FEED YOUR DOG PORK!" This is something that was told to me and my parents by none other than a veterinarian when I was a kid. So, I grew up thinking that there was something wrong with pork. Guess what? That myth is about as wrong as you can get.

The reality is that you shouldn't feed your dog *uncooked* pork. Uncooked pork can harbor *trichinosis*, a parasite, which is very dangerous to both people and dogs, which is why the FDA has drilled it into us to always cook pork. But this really doesn't explain what is wrong with giving pork to dogs.

The answer is: nothing. Pork can be a bit fatty—and if your dog is prone to developing pancreatitis due to overindulgence in fat, then maybe fatty pork isn't a good food for your dog (though lean pork is fine). Pork bones aren't great for dogs because they're sharp and can splinter, but for that matter neither are chicken bones, steak bones, or any bone that is sharp or that can be broken off and swallowed. In fact, you may be surprised to learn that some very premium dog food uses pork as a meat ingredient and that many disgustingly delightful dog chews are made from pig ears, pig snouts, and other porcine pieces.

So, what's up with the anti-pork sentiment? I honestly don't know. So, unless your dog eats only kosher foods, feeding him bits of cooked pork is OK. 🐾

Should you let your dog roam?

AT ONE TIME OR ANOTHER, people used to let their dogs run loose all the time. The idea was that the dogs needed "room to roam." Even now, there are people who allow their dogs to wander all over the place. Is this a good idea?

Of course not. Loose dogs are a menace to themselves and others. Dogs can chase wildlife, destroy property, threaten people, knock over garbage cans, and run in dangerous packs. On the flip side, a dog that is loose can get hit by traffic, eat dangerous or toxic things like rat poisons and anti-freeze, get lost or stolen, get shot at, or even fall victim to cruel and evil people bent on doing it harm.

If that's not enough to keep your dog behind a fence, consider that most municipalities have some sort of leash laws. Namely, if your dog is caught loose, he goes to the pound and you get a fine. Not worth the trouble, is it? 🐾

Can you use people shampoo on a dog?

PEOPLE SHAMPOO, DOG SHAMPOO. If you read books that dog writers write, you'd think you'd be hurting your dog by using people shampoo on a dog.

Well, sometimes. Let's say you're out of a pH-balanced dog shampoo, and all you have is the shampoo you washed your hair with. Your dog comes home dirty. Do you wait or use the shampoo?

Go ahead and use the shampoo, but don't use it all the time. A special pH-balanced shampoo for dogs won't dry out his skin and coat the way a human shampoo can. 🐾

Is homemade food good for my dog?

EVERYONE LOVES A HOME-COOKED MEAL—dogs included. So, what's wrong with you cooking for your dog every day?

You can do it, with some caveats. First of all, be aware that dog nutrition is different from people nutrition. Dogs need a certain amount of nutrients that are balanced. Too much or too little can be dangerous. In other words, just feeding your dog what you *think* is OK or on advice from anyone who doesn't have training in canine nutrition can be asking for trouble.

However, there's good news. There are plenty of books and special software out there to help you formulate your dog's diet and vitamin supplements made to balance your dog's food just right. Talking with a veterinary nutritionist is also a good idea. After all, if you're going through all that trouble to cook for your dog, you ought to at least make sure the diet is properly balanced. 🐾

Can steak bones kill my dog?

DOGS AND BONES: The two seem to go together. But you may have heard that steak bones can kill your dog. Is it just a rumor?

The problem is that cooked bones are harder and can splinter and break off easily. They can lodge in a dog's throat, and the sharp ones can perforate an intestine. In some cases, bones can block the intestine and cause serious problems that way.

So, that's cooked bones. What about raw bones? Well, the jury is still out on raw bones—and they're a fairly controversial topic. Raw bones can be softer and less dangerous than cooked bones, but may still present the problems associated with blockage. Even so, many people feed raw bones to their dogs all the time with certain raw food diets.

To be on the safe side, small, sharp bones and steak bones are definitely a no-no. Larger, meaty knucklebones are a bit safer as long as they're uncooked, but they can harbor bacteria. The choice is really up to you. 🐾

Can dogs and cats really get along?

YOU'VE PROBABLY HEARD THE ADAGE "fighting like cats and dogs." You've probably seen a dog chase a cat. There are often cat and dog owners. But will the twain ever meet?

According to the Pet Products Manufacturers Association, a full 45 percent of households own more than one pet, and 46 percent of dog owners own cats as well. That's a huge number, if you look at it. Certainly, dogs and cats can and do get along.

But don't take my word for it—check out your pet-owning friends who have cats and dogs. That alone should tell you that "fighting like cats and dogs" doesn't always happen, or does it? 🐾

Can people get worms from dogs?

THERE'S A LOT OF MISINFORMATION about worms and dogs. One old wives' tale has to do with getting pinworms from dogs. The good news is, you can't get pinworms from dogs—you get them from other people.

But what about other worms, such as roundworms, tapeworms, and hookworms?

Well, people can and do get roundworms, but quite often through poor hygiene (handling feces) or through eating dirt (yum!). Because humans aren't the right host for roundworms, they can cause havoc with a person's health, including blindness. (Isn't that wonderful?) Kids who eat dirt are often more susceptible.

Tapeworms are often contracted from eating raw, infected meat; or if you have fleas, from swallowing fleas. Hookworms can be contracted through piercing the skin (usually bare feet) and from oral contamination.

If you keep your dog worm-free and follow basic hygiene (washing hands before eating or touching your mouth), you're extremely unlikely to contract worms. Unless, of course, you just like the taste of dirt.... 🐾

Can you get a disease from your dog?

DISEASES THAT ARE TRANSMITTED from animals to humans are called *zoonotic diseases*. Zoonotic diseases are pretty rare, but occasionally do emerge. One well-publicized disease is rabies, which you can get if you're bitten by an infected dog.

But what about other diseases? Technically, although extremely rare, humans can get heartworm disease from infected mosquitoes. It's rare, but there has been talk about humans contracting leptospirosis from infected dogs (although it's more likely spread through contaminated water and rats). You actually can contract ringworm (not a worm at all, but a fungus) from a dog that has been infected (and therefore you're advised to wear rubber gloves when treating a pet).

Dogs can give you salmonella, tularemia, *E. coli,* or campylobacter if they eat raw meat and then lick your face or hands where you don't wash before you eat or if you have an open sore or wound. Although you're more likely to get toxoplasmosis from undercooked food or working in the garden, there's a chance of getting it from your dog (although once you've caught it, you'll never get it again). 🐾

Is chocolate really bad for dogs?

MAGGIE REMEMBERS A story in a book from when she was growing up about a kid who gave chocolate chips to a dog in order to make friends with it. The problem with the story is that chocolate is naturally bad for dogs. But you may be wondering, how bad?

Well, it depends on the type of chocolate and the size and sensitivity of the dog. Chocolate contains a chemical called *theobromine*, which is very similar to caffeine, both of which are toxic to dogs. Chocolate poisoning can start out with digestive problems such as vomiting, diarrhea, and gas. It can then progress to rapid, irregular heartbeat, hyperactivity, high blood pressure, tremors, seizures, respiratory failure, heart attack, and death. A very unpleasant way to go.

Humans can process theobromine well, but dogs cannot. So chocolate with high amounts of theobromine (the dark and bittersweet varieties) is much more dangerous to dogs than milk chocolate. Mild poisoning, according to the *Merck Veterinary Manual*, can occur at 0.32 ounces per pound of theobromine and caffeine and deadly results at over 0.64 ounces per pound of theobromine and caffeine, or about 6.4 ounces for a 10-pound dog. Even so, one ounce of milk chocolate per pound of dog can be lethal.

So skip the chocolate for Valentine's Day. Or at least, don't share it with your dog. 🐾

8

Q MORE CANINE QUESTIONS A

Do dogs have souls and do they go to heaven?

THIS IS ARGUABLY ONE OF THE QUESTIONS that will generate a fair amount of controversy for many years to come. In Christianity, especially Roman Catholicism, it was believed that animals—including dogs—don't have souls and therefore don't go to heaven. This doctrine has pretty much been St. Thomas Aquinas's doing, although some versions of Christianity are coming around to accepting dogs as having souls, thereby allowing them entry into heaven.

While the Catholic Church still wavers on its dog/soul/heaven questions, they do celebrate the feast day of St. Francis of Assisi with an annual blessing of the animals. Other religions, both past and present, do insist that animals (and therefore dogs) have souls. Hinduism, Shinto, Buddism, Pagan (e.g., Wicca), and many other religions all treat animals as having souls.

But do they really have souls? Do you have a soul? Do I have a soul? In truth, we may never know whether dogs have souls, at least while we are still alive.

Do all dogs come from wolves?

GIVEN ALL THE CANINE VARIATIONS ONE SEES—from the tiniest Chihuahua to the greatest of Great Danes—people have often wondered whether dogs came from something other than wolves. One thing that DNA research has proven beyond a shadow of a doubt is that all dogs are descended from wolves—in particular, the Asian wolf.

Scientists studied the DNA of 654 dogs, which indicate that dogs not only originated from wolves, but did so from wolves from a specific area, namely East Asia. Dogs that came with humans over the Bering land bridge are believed to have been the ancestors of dogs in the New World.

Can human infants be raised by wolves?

THE STORIES ABOUT CHILDREN BEING raised by wolves are almost as old as humanity. The concept of a child being abandoned and being taken in by wolves or other species is an appealing narrative and one that people enjoy retelling. Perhaps the most famous of these stories is that of Romulus and Remus, the legendary founders of Rome. But how true are these stories—and can human children actually be raised by wolves?

The answer may surprise you. Although rare, there have been cases of children found in the wild who are feral. According to one Internet site which documents cases (www.feralchildren.com), at times children have been raised by wolves, dogs, apes, bears, monkeys, sheep, goats, and cows. How many of these stories are true rather than legend is another matter altogether.

Interestingly enough, once a child is raised by another animal, the child is severely developmentally handicapped. The child will often behave like its foster parents (in the case of wolves, growling, biting, snarling, and running on all fours). The child can almost never learn to speak or fit into society. So, while the wolf may have done the child a favor by saving its life, the child is doomed to a wolflike existence. 🐾

Do dogs see ghosts?

SINCE NEITHER CAROLINE NOR MAGGIE believe in ghosts, this question was especially hard for us to answer. However, Maggie has a friend, the world-famous cat author and ghost expert Dusty Rainbolt, author of *Ghost Cats: Human Encounters with Feline Spirits* and *Cat Wrangling Made Easy* (Lyons Press). Dusty does a fair amount of ghost hunting in her spare time and has seen some pretty odd stuff. So what does she think about ghosts and dogs?

"Yes, I definitely think that dogs can sense ghosts because they have more acute senses than people. They can see in the dark better and, because they can sense changes in magnetic fields and have more sensitive hearing, they're bound to notice ghosts," Dusty says. "It works on the same principle as animals that disappear before an earthquake. There were very few animals that died in the tsunami in 2005 because they sensed it and went to higher ground. It's the same principle. Animals have more awareness of things around them."

So, there you have it. If there are ghosts, you can bet your dog has encountered a couple. 🐾

Are dogs psychic?

YOU'RE ABOUT TO LEAVE ON A TRIP FOR A FEW DAYS. Before you know it, your dog is moping around the house or acting anxious because he knows he's going to the kennel. Is he psychic? Does he know when things are going to happen before they do?

Before you start naming your dog the Great Karnack, you might consider a dog's amazing power of observation that would put Sherlock Holmes to shame. Dogs, being predators, are great observers and know the subtle signs that indicate when you're going on a trip, even before you pack your bags. Your dog notices the frequency of phone calls, your demeanor, your smell and mood, and other things that have cued him off in the past that you're leaving.

Your dog isn't psychic. He's just very good at recognizing the signs of things to come. 🐾

Do people whip sled dogs to make them run?

WE'VE ALL SEEN THE OLD VIDEOS of the musher (sled-dog driver) cracking the whip to get his huskies to go faster. But do mushers whip their dogs to make them run? And why do they use whips anyway?

Sled dogs run because they love to do so. They are trained for three hundred to a thousand miles each year before they ever get to run their first sprint, and over a thousand miles before running a long-distance race. Dogs that do not love to run don't make the team.

In the past, mushers took their cues from mule drivers, using whips and commands to train dogs. In the recent past, mushers have used what is called a *signal whip*—that is, a whip that is about a yard long—and popped it to signal the team to speed up. These whips are too short to reach even the back dogs on a team, so there was no possible way a musher could actually hit a dog with the whip.

Nowadays most races ban the use of whips because of the bad image they have. Mushers use training and positive techniques to get their dogs to run. In extremely rare circumstances, there have been bad apples in mushing (just as there are bad dog owners everywhere), but in most instances mushers try to do what is best for their dogs, including giving them proper nutrition, exercise, training, and attention. 🐾

Do dogs really resemble their owners?

WE'VE ALL SEEN PHOTOS of owners and their dogs, maybe on TV or in a newspaper, and gotten a good chuckle at dogs and owners who resemble each other. But do such odd couplings actually occur in real life?

Well, guess what? There's been a study to determine just that. And, oddly enough, the answer is most decidedly "yes!" Researchers at the University of California, San Diego, studied forty-five dogs and their owners. They had judges come in and look at a photo of the owner and then look at pictures of the owner's dog and another dog. In most cases, the judges could correctly pick out the right dog. The results were published in the journal *Psychological Science*.

What's interesting is that the positive results were confined to purebreds rather than mixed breeds, suggesting that people select a certain look that appeals to them. As for the authors looking like our dogs, well... 🐾

How many people are bitten by dogs every year?

IT'S ESTIMATED THAT approximately 4 million people are bitten each year by dogs (or about 1.3 percent of the U.S. population), according to the Centers for Disease Control and Prevention (CDC). 🐾

Why do dogs bite people?

MOST BITES ARE NOT SERIOUS and are never reported, but about 400,000 are. You may be wondering why dogs bite people.

Well, the answer is complex, but most dogs bite out of fear, pain, dominance, guarding, or frustration. A few dogs bite because they are sick or have some sort of condition that causes them to bite.

Let's look at sick dogs first. Dogs with rabies and other diseases may bite someone. Likewise, a dog with a congenital condition called *idiopathic aggression* (sometimes called rage or Springer rage syndrome) may have a seizure that triggers aggression and attack without provocation. Luckily, this condition is rare.

Normal dogs may bite for a variety of reasons, but many bite on account of pain (injury) or fear (being put in a scary situation or made to do something they don't want to). Truly aggressive dogs may be aggressive because they're trying to show you who is dominant, i.e., who's boss.

An aggressive dog may be guarding territory or a particular piece of property (like food) and may bite if you try to take the food away. Lastly, there's a type of aggression call frustration, in which the dog is unable to take out his aggressions on what is making him angry and so bites the nearest available victim (such as the dog seeing another dog he hates and bites you because he can't get to the dog).

Other types of aggression include sexual aggression (but it seldom leads to people getting bit) and maternal aggression (where you threaten a dam's pups).

Dogs bite mainly because there is usually something causing them to bite. In most cases, it's a situation where the dog wants you to understand, in no uncertain terms, to go away. There are always exceptions to this rule, but keeping your distance and leaving a stray dog alone is always a good idea. 🐾

What's the ugliest dog?

AT THE SONOMA-MARIN FAIR in Petaluma, California, Sam the Chinese Crested won the World's Ugliest Dog Contest in 2005 at the ripe old age of fourteen. However, due to age-related illnesses, Sam passed away later that year. The next year, the title was won by another Chinese Crested named Archie. And while Archie is no beauty queen, we have to agree that Sam is, so far, the all-time ugliest dog. 🐾

What's the prettiest dog?

BEAUTY IS CERTAINLY IN THE EYE OF THE BEHOLDER, so it's tough for us to truly say who exactly is the prettiest dog. But if you want showstoppers, take a look at the Westminster Kennel Club winners. The judges chose Ch Felicity's Diamond Jim, aka Jim, an English Springer Spaniel, as being the dog that most conformed to the standard.

But we all know that judge was wrong, wrong, wrong. The prettiest dog is the one at my side. And the one at yours. 🐾

Who was the oldest dog?

According to *The Guinness Book of World Records*, the oldest dog was a black Labrador Retriever named Adjutant who lived to be a bit over twenty-seven-years-old. 🐾

How hard is the average dog bite?

FOUR HUNDRED POUNDS per square inch. That's bone-crushing, in case you were wondering. 🐾

How many people are killed by dogs every year?

TEN TO TWENTY ON AVERAGE. When you calculate that the number of dogs is over 73 million in the United States alone (at least according to the American Pet Products Manufacturers Association), this is a very small incidence. More people are killed by deer than by dogs. 🐾

Will plastic jugs filled with water keep dogs from pooping on your lawn?

NOT UNLESS YOU cover your entire lawn with them. 🐾

Is cocoa mulch harmful to pets?

A PRODUCT NOW AVAILABLE in lawn and garden shops is cocoa bean shell mulch. It's biodegradable and uses products that would normally be thrown away. But is it safe for pets?

The answer is, no. Cocoa mulch is highly toxic to pets because it contains high amounts of theobromine, the same toxin found in chocolate.

So, skip the cocoa mulch and use bark if you must mulch. 🐾

Can dogs get the plague?

WE'VE ALL HEARD ABOUT BUBONIC PLAGUE (the Black Death) from history books, but you might not know that canines are resistant to plague.

Plague is caused by the bacteria *Yersinia pestis* and is carried by fleas on rodents. Animals, such as cats, can become infected with it by eating infected rodents. However, most canine species, including foxes and coyotes, usually do not suffer from the plague or may experience only undetectable symptoms of it. So, most dogs will not show signs of plague infection.

However, if your dog is exposed to the plague, you can still contract it from him, which is why it is important to stay away from rodents in plague areas such as the western United States. 🐾

Does the black pigment on the roof of a dog's mouth indicate anything?

THIS IS ONE OF THOSE MYTHS I GREW UP WITH—that if a dog had black pigment inside the roof of its mouth, it meant that the dog was of good temperament. Other similar statements opine that black pigment in the mouth means the dog is purebred. Well, like most old wives' tales, this one's hogwash (or dogwash). Here's why.

First, there's temperament: There's no conclusive evidence that black pigment inside a dog's mouth means anything more than that it has black pigment inside its mouth. As far as temperament is concerned, dogs with black mouths have bitten me, so there goes that myth right out the window.

What about being purebred? Well, I've owned plenty of mixed breeds that had black pigment inside their mouths. What's more, I own a purebred that had a black mouth and that lost her oral pigment for some reason and now has a pink mouth. So, that's clearly not an indication of being purebred either. (And, by the way, she really has a great personality.)

Dogs that have black pigment in their mouths may be purebred or mixed breed, smart or dumb, and may have a good or bad temperament. Pigment means little save in the cosmetics department, unless it has something to do with a health condition.

So, why is there this myth about pigment in a dog's mouth? I don't know. My dogs don't seem to notice or care either. 🐾

9

DOG BREEDS

Are Malamutes or Huskies "wild" dogs?

WHEN MAGGIE WAS GROWING UP, she heard all about these "wild" dogs of the north. You know—the Malamutes and Huskies. But are these dogs really wild?

Alaskan Malamutes and Siberian Huskies are two dog breeds whose roots go back to antiquity. That means that genetically, these dogs were some of the very first that people domesticated when they got around to domesticating dogs. What's more, researchers tested Siberian Huskies and Alaskan Malamutes and found that 100 percent of their behavior matched wolf behavior.

And yet, despite their so-called wolflike appearance and behavior, these creatures are dogs, not wolves. They were bred for a specific purpose by Inuits: to pull a sled. They bond with humans just like other dogs and prefer being in the company of people rather than out on their own.

So, no, Malamutes and Huskies aren't "wild" dogs—no matter how wild they act! 🐾

Do some dog breeds have wolf in them?

YOU LOOK AT SOME DOGS and swear you're encountering a wolf. But is it a wolf? Do some dog breeds have wolf in them?

Well, yes, all dog breeds have wolf in them. Dogs were domesticated from wolves, so when you look into those loving eyes, you see a wolf staring back at you. A domesticated wolf, but nevertheless, a wolf.

Oh, you mean a dog breed with wolf recently added? Well, there are dogs that are called wolf hybrids, and these dogs do indeed have wolf in them, but they do not make up a breed. Then, there are some unusual breeds that do have wolf in them, including the Czechoslovakian Wolfdog and the Saarloos Wolfhound, both of which were developed fairly recently using wolf stock. 🐾

What's the oldest breed of dog?

YOU WANT TO PICK A FIGHT? Try walking into a dog show and declaring that your dog is the oldest breed. I guarantee, them be fightin' words.

Almost every breed claims to have ancient origins, but the proof has come from none other than genetics. Using what are called microsatellite markers—segments of nuclear DNA that vary greatly among different dogs but tend to be the same in closely related individuals—researchers could make inferences about their relationships between breeds and, more importantly for this question, different breeds and wolves. Of the eighty-five breeds tested, they found a cluster of breeds that appeared to be closely related to ancestral wolf types. These breeds formed branches which may have then led to other breeds. These branches and their breeds were as follows: (1) the Chinese Shar-pei, Shiba Inu, Akita, and Chow Chow; (2) the Basenji; (3) the Alaskan Malamute and Siberian Husky; and (4) the Afghan Hound and Saluki. By changing some parameters slightly, the Tibetan Terrier, Lhasa Apso, Pekingese, Shih Tzu, and Samoyed also made the grade. The fact that this progenitor cluster derives from a broad geographic expanse suggests that the first dogs originated in Asia and migrated with humans throughout Asia, as far north as the Arctic, and as far south as Africa.

The remaining breeds (those not in this progenitor cluster) probably originated more recently from a European matrix. Applying more sensitive analyses allows these breeds to be subdivided into three groups. The first is made up of Mastiff-like breeds that include the Boxer, Bulldog, Newfoundland, and other guarding dogs. The German Shepherd also falls into this group, perhaps reflecting an influx of genes from military dogs with Mastiff forebears. A second subdivision is made up of herding-type breeds such as the Collie,

Belgian Sheepdog, and Australian Shepherd. This group also surprisingly contained the Saint Bernard, Greyhound, Borzoi, and Irish Wolfhound. These latter nonherding breeds may have been either herding breed progenitors or descendents of the same. The remaining subdivision represents a wide variety of dogs of mostly recent European descent and includes terriers, scent hounds, spaniels, pointers, and retrievers.

So while only a handful of breeds can claim bragging rights as original dogs, don't despair: The others can proudly wear the label "new and improved." 🐾

Can Poodles run the Iditarod?

THERE'S THAT POODLE QUESTION AGAIN! One man, John Suter, ran Standard Poodles in four Iditarods from 1988 to 1991. According to Suter, his dogs finished midpack in the race each time. 🐾

What breeds of dog make up sled dogs?

MOST PEOPLE, when they see sled dogs, think Siberian Huskies, Alaskan Malamutes, or even Samoyeds. And they'd be correct, but there are plenty of other dogs that have made the list of sled dogs.

The least and the best known are the mixed-breed dogs that run sled-dog races such as the Iditarod, Yukon Quest, and others. These dogs are called Alaskan Huskies and are a mix of various fast dogs (Husky, Malamute, Pointer, and Hound crosses). These dogs are bred for speed, not looks.

But there are other dogs that have pulled sleds as well. Targhee Hounds, named for the forest in Idaho, were a mixture of Setters and Greyhounds that raced for years. There's a particular strain of Alaskan Huskies called Aurora Huskies (Wright Hounds) that were Huskies bred with Setters. In addition, there are Inuit Dogs

(Canadian Eskimo Dogs) and Mackenzie River Huskies, both sizable animals intended for pulling large loads.

Nowadays, mushers have run Dalmatians, Labrador Retrievers, Irish Setters, German Shorthaired Pointers, English Shorthaired Pointers, and a variety of those mixes. If it's a dog, it's probably had a harness strapped on it at one time or another. 🐾

What's the most popular dog breed?

LABRADOR RETRIEVERS, according to the American Kennel Club (AKC). 🐾

Are Cockapoos, Peekapoos, and other designer dogs breeds?

YOU'VE SEEN THOSE FANCY-SCHMANCY designer dogs with the high price tags. Maybe you have one of them. You may be wondering what all the fuss is about these dogs and whether they are purebreds.

Not exactly. A dog breed consists of at least seven generations of dogs in which the animals come from the same breed and have enough individuals around in different regions to be considered a viable breed. So, dogs that are crossbred, for example, whose parents are a Cocker Spaniel and a Poodle, aren't purebred. They're a crossbreed or a mixed breed.

That doesn't mean that these dogs can't be purebred down the road, if they meet the criteria of kennel clubs such as the AKC and the United Kennel Club; but for the moment, these dogs are not considered purebred. 🐾

Why are Dalmatians associated with fire departments?

You've seen those spotted, trustworthy companions of fire departments everywhere. They're a tradition, but I bet you don't know why. It took a bit of digging to find out, and the truth turns out to be stranger than fiction.

Dalmatians were often known as *carriage dogs*, meaning that they did well running beside horses. But that's not why they're firehouse dogs. You see, there was this guy named Benjamin Franklin (yeah, the same guy on the hundred dollar bill), who in between writing his *Poor Richard's Almanac*, discovering electricity, and rabble-rousing the United States into the Revolutionary War, bred Dalmatians. Ben also started the very first fire department in the New World.

Now, a clever guy like Ben figured out that (being the entrepreneurial type) he could provide Dalmatians as mascots for his fire departments (Dalmatians do have big litters), and the Dalmatian became the mascot for fire departments everywhere. This isn't a bad deal for either the Dalmatian or the firefighters. The firefighters get a loyal, trustworthy companion, and the Dalmatians get yummy meals, lots of love, and the admiration of schoolchildren everywhere.

That Ben Franklin guy was pretty clever. 🐾

INDEX

Age, dog years vs. people years, 86–87
Aggression. *See also* Biting
  from birth, 23
  people killed by, 162
  predatory instinct and, 5–6, 146
  sucking food and, 6
  types of, 160–161
Albinos, 58–59
Alcohol, dogs and, 145
Allergies
  dogs with, 71
  people with, dogs good for, 88–89
  shedding and, 90–91
Alpha rolling, 12
Alzheimer's, 45–46
Amnesia, 26
Anal sacs, 18
Anosmia, 102
Balls, why dogs like, 31
Barking
  debarking surgery and, 8
  reasons for, 6–8
Baths, 29–30, 150
Behavior of dogs. *See also* Aggression;
Barking; Biting; Emotions; Reactions
of dogs; Smelling and sniffing
  alpha rolling and, 12
  amnesia and, 26
  burying bones, 16–17
  chasing things, 4–5
  circling before lying down, 20–21
  cocking head, 18–19
  cocking leg, 9–10
  compulsive behaviors, 16, 23–24, 25
  eating plants, dirt, and other weird
    stuff, 15–16
  eating poop, 14–15
  fear of thunder, 21–22
  hanging head out car window,
    25–26
  howling with sirens, 21
  hypnosis and, 27–28
  jumping on people, 11

  killing animals and turning on
    people, 5–6, 146
  knowing it's time for walk, 30–31
  knowing when to eat, 30
  licking people, 11
  liking balls, 31
  narcolepsy, 26–27
  peeing habits. *See* Peeing
  rubbing on disgusting stuff, 17
  scooting butt on ground, 18
  wagging tail, 19
  yawning, 13
Belly buttons, 65
Bestiality, 133–134
Biting. *See also* Aggression
  alpha rolling and, 12
  danger of, varying with dog, 76
  own tongue, 75
  reasons for, 160–161
  statistics on, 160, 162
Blindness, 113–114
Blood donors, 94–95
Blood types, 95
Blushing, 57
Bobtailed dogs, 85–86
Bonding, with older dogs, 143–144
Bones, burying, 16–17
Bones, safety of, 149, 151–152
Borborygmi, 69
Breath, of dogs, 142
Breeds, 166–170
  bite danger and, 76
  designer dogs and, 169
  DNA tests and, 128
  dogs resembling owners, 159–160
  intelligence tendencies, 37–40
  most popular, 169
  oldest, 167–168
  wolves and. *See* Wolves
Burying bones, 16–17
Butts, scooting on ground, 18
Butts, sniffing, 13
Calcium, giving to pregnant dog, 134

Cancer, in dogs, 48, 59, 132
Cancer, sniffing out, 101–102
Canine transmissible venereal tumor (CTVT), 132
Canine viral papillomas, 64
Cars
  chasing, 4–5
  hanging head out window, 25–26
  loving or hating rides in, 145–146
Cataracts, 112–113
Cat food, 148
Cats
  chasing, reasons for, 4
  dogs getting along with, 152
  hair balls and, 66
  with six toes, 80
Chasing other things, 4–5
Chasing own tail, 24–25
Chocolate precaution, 153–154
Circling before lying down, 20–21
Cloned dogs, 137–139
Cocking head, 18–19
Cocking leg, 9–10
Cocoa mulch, 162
Colds, 67
Collarbones, 70
Color perception, 107–108
Comatose dogs, 28–29
Compulsive behaviors, 16, 23–24, 25
Conjoined dogs, 129
Convulsing. See Seizures
Coprophagy (eating doo-doo), 14–15
Counting skills, 41–42
Coyotes, dogs and, 6, 7, 54, 131, 162–163
Crying, 52
C-sections, 135
Dalmatians, deafness and, 76, 114, 115–116
Dalmatians, firehouses and, 115–116, 170
Deaf dogs, 76, 114, 115–116
Debarking surgery, 8
Designer dogs, 169
Digestive problems, 15, 69. See also Food and diet
Dirt, eating, 15–16
Disease, contracting from dog, 153
DNA testing, 126–127, 128

Docked tails, 20, 82–85
"Dog-appeasing pheromones," 105
Ears, cropping, 117
Eggs, 144
Embarrassment, 53–54, 57
Emotions, 48–54
  after baths, 29–30
  compulsive behaviors and, 16, 23–24, 25
  crying and, 52
  embarrassment and, 53–54, 57
  falling in love and, 51–52
  friends, enemies and, 50
  hugging and, 29
  jealousy and spite, 50–51
  mourning, 48
  sense of humor, practical jokes and, 53
  trancing and, 28
  trust issues (dog, others, and you) and, 48–49
Enemies and friends, 50
Eyelid, third, 113
Eyes
  blue, causes and associations, 76–77
  closed at birth, 119–120
  colors of, 76–77
  glowing when angry, 108–109
  pepper spray in, 106–107
  popping out, 65–66
  of puppies, 119–121
  reflective nature of, 77
  third eyelid and, 113
Eyesight
  cataracts, replacement lenses and, 112–113
  color perception, 107–108
  coping with blindness, 113–114
  with fur over eyes, 109
  nearsightedness, farsightedness, glasses and, 109–111
  of puppies, 120–121
  quality and physiology of, 107
  seeing pictures of dogs as real dogs, 2–3
  typical vision, 109
  varying by breed, 111

watching TV and, 111–112
False pregnancies, 135–137
Farts, 68–69
Fear, smelling, 98
Feet
    extra toes, 80
    purpose of footpad on wrist
        (stopper pad), 79–80
    running on snow, 92–93
    webbed, 80
Flu, 67–68
Foaming at mouth, 56–57, 106
Food and diet
    alcohol and, 145
    cat food, 148
    chocolate precaution, 153–154
    eating garbage, 143
    eating onions, 148–149
    eating plants, dirt, and other weird
        stuff, 15–16
    eating poop and, 14–15
    eggs, 144
    gas and, 68–69
    homemade food, 151
    intelligence and, 44
    knowing when to eat, 30, 69
    long-distance racing and, 94
    low blood sugar and, 73–74
    pork, 149–150
    sense of taste and, 117–118, 120
    sucking food instead of lapping, 6
    sweeteners, 72–73, 118
    table scraps, 144–145
    treats, 41–42, 144–145
Foxes, dogs and, 6, 15, 131, 162–163
Friends and enemies, 50
Fur
    bundles of hair, 89–90
    eggs being god for, 144
    gray, 58
    hair balls, 66
    over eyes, 109
    shaving, effects of, 60–61
    shedding or not, 90–91
    single- and double-coated dogs,
        89–90, 91–92
Garbage, eating, 143

Gas, 68–69
Ghosts, dogs seeing, 157–158
Goose bumps, 63–64
Grass, eating, 15
Hair. See Fur
Head
    black pigment in mouths, 163
    cocking, 18–19
    hanging out car window, 25–26
    phrenology and, 36
    size, intelligence and, 35–36
Hearing
    cropping ears and, 117
    deafness and, 76, 114, 115–116
    dog whistles and, 116
    of puppies, 121
    testing, 114
    ultrasonic pest deterrents and,
        116–117
Hearing aids, 114–115
Heaven, dogs and, 156
Herpes, 132–133
Hiccups, 71–72
Hiking leg, 9–10
Hip dysplasia, 81–82
Homosexuality, 124
Howling with sirens, 21
Hugging dogs, 29
Hunting. See Predatory instinct
Huskies, 92–93, 128, 158–159, 166, 167,
    168–169
Hydrophobia, 56
Hypnosis, 27–28
Hypoglycemia (low blood sugar), 73–74
Idiopathic aggression, 160
Iditarod. See Sled dogs
Intelligence
    Alzheimer's and, 45–46
    breed tendencies, 37–40
    conscious thought and, 34–35
    counting skills, 41–42
    diet and, 44
    head/brain size and, 35–36
    instinctive math skills, 42
    learning to read, 43
    memory and, 37
    mental deficiencies, 40–41

Intelligence, *cont.*
  phrenology and, 36
  understanding pointing and, 42–43
  understanding time and, 45
Jackals, dogs and, 131
Jealousy and spite, 50–51
Jumping on people, 11
Left-pawed dogs, 69–70
Legs. *See also* Feet
  cocking, reasons for, 9–10
  falling asleep, 72
  missing, mobility when, 81
  purpose of footpad on wrist
    (stopper pad), 79–80
Licking
  people, reasons for, 10–11
  spit, germs and, 87–88
Litters
  conjoined puppies, 129
  C-sections for, 135
  identical twins, 128–129
  with multiple fathers, 125–126
  runts, 129–130
  sensory perception of puppies,
    119–121
Long-distance races, 93–94
Loose dogs, 150
Love, dogs in, 51–52
Low blood sugar, 73–74
Malamutes, 2, 7, 37, 53, 128, 166, 167, 168
Mating. *See* Sexual issues
Memory, 37
Mental illness, 22–23
Mirrors, reaction to, 3
Mouths, black pigment in, 163
Mulch precaution, 162
Name, changing, 143
Narcolepsy, 26–27
Nasal solar dermatitis, 59
Neoteny, 7, 143
Nictitating membrane, 113
Noses
  boogers and, 70–71
  sense of smell and. *See* Smelling and
    sniffing
  wet, reasons for, 70
Object permanence, 34

Obsessive-compulsive dogs, 23–24
Older dogs, bonding with, 143–144
Oldest dog, 161
Onions, eating, 148–149
Opponent process theory of emotion,
  30
Owners, dogs resembling, 159–160
Panting, 61–62
Paws. *See* Feet
Peeing. *See also* Urine
  cocking leg and, 9–10
  in fear, 21
  in house, 50, 89
  information in urine and, 13–14
  jealousy, spite and, 50–51
Pepper spray, 106–107
Pheromones, 105, 106
Phrenology, 36
Pica, 16
Pictures, as real dogs, 2–3
Pimples, 63
Plague, 162–163
Plants, eating, 15–16
Pointing, understanding, 42–43
Poodles, 2, 3, 38, 43, 88–89, 90, 168
Poop
  eating, reasons for, 14–15
  information in urine and, 13–14
  people getting worms from, 152–153
  plastic jugs on lawn and, 162
  sniffing, of other dogs, 13–14
Pork, for dogs, 149–150
Practical jokes, 53
Predatory instinct
  disguising scent to hunt and, 17
  living with dogs and, 5–6, 146
  why dogs chase cats and, 4
Pregnancy. *See* Litters; Sexual issues
Prettiest dog, 161
Proptosis, 65–66
Psychic dogs, 158
Puppies. *See* Litters
Rabid dogs, 56–57
Racing, long-distance, 93–94
Reactions of dogs
  to cars, 4–5, 145–146
  to cats, 4

to hugging, 29
to mirrors, 3
to other dogs' pee, 106
to people, if dog kills animals,
5–6, 146
to pictures of dogs, 2–3
to Poodles, 2
Reading, teaching, 43
Retrograde amnesia, 26
Right-pawed dogs, 69–70
Roaming dogs, 150
Rocks, eating, 15–16
Rolling dog over (alpha rolling), 12
Rubbing on disgusting stuff, 17
Runts, 129–130
Sadness, 48
Seeing. See Eyes; Eyesight
Seizures
    duration of, 74
    idiopathic aggression and, 160
    low blood sugar and, 73
    in people, dogs recognizing, 103–104
    trancing and, 28
    treating, 74
Senility, 45–46
Sense of humor, 53
Senses. See Eyes; Eyesight; Hearing;
    Smelling and sniffing; Taste, sense of;
    Touch, whiskers and
Sensitivity, of perception, 158
Sexual issues, 124–139. See also Litters
    being stuck (tied) during inter-
        course, 124–125
    big and little dogs mating, 130–131
    breeding considerations, 129–130
    cloning dogs and, 137–139
    DNA testing and, 126–128
    falling in love and, 51–52
    false pregnancies, 135–137
    giving calcium to pregnant dog, 134
    homosexuality, 124
    human and dog sexual relations,
        133–134
    intercourse, 124–125
    mating with other animals, 131
    ovulation cycle, 130
    paternity testing, 126–127

sniffing other dogs' butts and, 13
sniffing pee of another dog, chomp-
    ing, foaming at mouth and, 106
vomeronasal organ and, 14, 106
Sexually transmitted diseases (STDs),
    132–133
Shampoo, for dogs, 150
Shaving dogs, 60–61
Shedding, 90–91
Sirens, howling with, 21
Skunk odor, removing, 147
Sled dogs
    breeds of, 168–169
    endurance factors, 93–94
    Poodles as, 168
    sleeping/running in snow without
        freezing, 91–93
    whipping, 158–159
Sleep(ing)
    legs falling asleep, 72
    snoring and, 72
    in snow without freezing, 91–92
Smelling and sniffing
    cancer, 101–102
    difference between identical twins,
        98–99
    "dog-appeasing pheromones" and,
        105
    fear, 98
    losing ability of, 102
    other dogs' butts, 13
    other dogs' pee or poop, 13–14, 106
    physiology of, 104–105
    prenatal, 121
    by puppies, 120, 121
    sensitivity of, 104–105
    tracking odor trails, 99–100
    wet noses and, 70
Snoring, 72
Snow. See Sled dogs
Socks, eating, 17
Souls, dogs and, 156
Speed, of dogs, 79
Spit, germs in, 87–88
Sugar, dogs and, 72–73
Sunburn, 59
Sweating, 61–63

Sweets, dogs and, 72–73, 118
Swimming, 78
Table scraps, 144–145
Tails
    bobtailed dogs, 85–86
    chasing, reasons for, 24–25
    docked, 20, 82–85
    wagging, 19
Tapetum, 77, 108–109
Taste, sense of, 117–118, 120
Tears, 52
Television, dogs watching, 111–112
Temperature, body, 61–63
    normal range, 60
    regulating, 61–63, 120
    shaving fur and, 60–61
    sweating, panting and, 61–63
Theobromine, 154, 162
Thinking, 34–35. *See also* Intelligence
Thunder, fear of, 21–22
Tickling dogs, 71
Time(ing)
    dogs understanding, 30–31, 45
    dog years vs. people years, 86–87
Toes, extra, 80
Toilets, drinking from, 142
Tongue
    biting, 75
    licking people, 10–11
    living without, 75
    swallowing, seizures and, 74
Tonic recumbency, 27–28
Tonsillitis, 66–67
Touch, whiskers and, 118–119
Tracking odor trails, 99–100
Training, breed intelligence and, 37–40
Trancing, 28
Treats, 41–42, 144–145
Trust issues (dog, others, and you),
    48–49
Twins (identical)
    dogs as, 128–129
    dogs smelling difference between,
    98–99

Ugliest dog, 161
Umbilical hernias, 65
Urine
    allergies to, 89
    brown, eating onions and, 148–149
    information in, 13–14
    organ forcing sample of into mouth,
    106
    smelling cancer in, 101–102
    smelling, then chomping, foaming
    at mouth, 106
    sniffing, 13–14, 106
Vibrissae (whiskers), 118–119
Vomeronasal organ, 14, 106
Wagging tail, 19
Warts, 64
Whiskers, 118–119
Whistles, "silent," 116
Wolves
    alpha rolling and, 12
    barking and, 6–8
    breeds more similar/related to, 38,
    166, 167
    breeds with wolf in them, 166
    in dog breeds, 166
    dogs mating with, 131
    dogs originating from, 156
    eating plants, 15
    howling, 21
    hunting instinct, 146
    juvenile, dogs as (neoteny), 7, 143
    mating habits, 51
    pointing and, 49
    raising human babies, 157
    wagging tails, 19
Worms, contracting from dog, 152–153
Worms, dogs with, 18
Yawning, 13
Years, dog vs. people, 86–87

About the Authors

D. CAROLINE COILE, PhD, has written 29 books and more than 300 magazine and scientific article about dogs. She's a columnist for *Dog World* magazine, and her dog writing awards include the Dog Writers' Association of America's Maxwell Award (seven times), Denlinger Award, the Eukanuba Canine Health Award (twice), and AKC Canine Health Foundation Award (twice). Among her favorite books are her *Encyclopedia of Dog Breeds* (Barron''s Educational Series), *How Smart Is Your Dog?* (Sterling Publishing), *Congratulations! It's a Dog!* (Barron''s Educational Series), and *Silly Dog Tricks* (Sterling Publishing).

Caroline's research and teaching interests revolve around canine behavior, senses, and genetics. She has served as a canine consultant to the FAA and is on the AKC Canine Health Foundation President's Council. She has appeared on many television and radio shows talking, of course, about dogs.

On a practical level, Caroline has lived with dogs all her life. They have included nationally ranked show, field, obedience, and agility dogs, which regularly pull her away from her desk, and her writing. They also seem to have conspired to convince her ona daily basis that she knows absolutely nothing about dogs!

MARGARET H. BONHAM (Maggie) is a world-renowned pet expert and award-winning author of 28 books and hundreds of articles about dogs and cats. Her writing awards have included the Dog Writers' Association of America's Maxwell Award (three times), the Pet Sitters' International First Canine Award, and second place in the 2005 Preditors and Editors People's Choice Awards. She is the author of many pet books including *Introduction to Dog Agility* (Barron's Educational Series), *A Dog's Wisdom* and *The Complete Guide to Mutts* (Howell Book House), and *The Pocket Idiot's Guide to Homemade Dog Food* (Alpha Books).

Maggie is a member of the Dog Writers' Association of America and the Cat Writers' Association. A pet behaviorist, she has been a member of the Association of Pet Dog Trainers (APDT), and trained over 50 dogs in obedience, agility, backpacking, and sledding sports. She has appeared on dozens of radio programs and in hundreds of magazines and newspapers as a pet expert. Her writing has appeared in *Prevention Magazine, Dog Fancy, Dog World, Mushing Magazine* and has been syndicated across the Internet through various newspapers.

Maggie has lived with and trained dogs all her life, choosing to work with the more difficult Northern Breeds and earning titles on her dogs in agility, backpacking, and sledding. When not working with dogs or cats, she writes science fiction and fantasy including *Prophecy of Swords, Runestone of Teiwas, Lachlei, The King's Champion*, and the upcoming werewolf thriller *Howling Dead*.